·TESCO· COOKERY· COLLECTION·

DAIRY COOKING
A HEALTHY APPROACH

Recipes written and developed by Lorna Rhodes with additional recipes by Claire Valentine
Additional assistance from the Tesco Consumer Kitchens

Published exclusively for Tesco Stores Ltd,
Delamare Road, Cheshunt, Herts EN8 9SL
by Cathay Books, 59 Grosvenor Street, London W1

First published 1987

© Cathay Books 1987

ISBN 0 86178 466 9

Printed in Hong Kong

ACKNOWLEDGEMENTS

The publishers would like to thank the following
who were concerned in the preparation of the book.

Series Art Director Pedro Prá-Lopez
Art Editor David Rowley
Series Editor Camilla Simmons
Photographer Chris Crofton
Stylist Maria Kelly
Food prepared for photography by Lorna Rhodes, Dolly Meers and Claire Valentine
Special editorial help Cathy Dunn

Introduction written by Kate Moseley

CONTENTS

NOTE

Standard spoon measurements are used in all recipes

1 tablespoon (tbls) = one 15 ml spoon
1 teaspoon (tsp) = one 5 ml spoon
All spoon measures are level

All eggs are sized 3 or 4 (standard) unless otherwise stated.

For all recipes, quantities are given in both metric and imperial measures. Follow either set but not a mixture of both, as they are not interchangeable.

Following the success of the first 20 books we produced in the Tesco Cookery Collection, we are delighted to be adding 4 new titles to this exciting series. As before, it is the close contact we have with our customers and the feedback we have had through our Consumer Advisory Kitchens which has helped us to select these latest titles. Each one focuses on an area in which our customers have shown particular interest and contains practical background information on the chosen subject together with a wide selection of carefully tested recipes, each one illustrated in colour.

Dairy products are natural and nutritious foods which can play a useful role in our lives as part of a balanced diet. The recipes in *Dairy Cooking* illustrate the many uses of dairy products from soups and starters to light desserts and dairy drinks. At the same time these dishes have been developed to suit today's style of healthy eating which means using dairy foods in moderation. This doesn't mean that the dishes are any less interesting or enjoyable just that they are a little less rich. I hope you will enjoy looking through these pages and trying out the recipes with your family and friends.

Carey Dennis, Head of Product and Consumer Services at Tesco

INTRODUCTION

Dairy products have a great place in today's healthy living as part of a balanced diet. They are natural foods that make eating a pleasure. The secret of getting the balance right is to use dairy products like butter and double cream where the flavour and texture are vital to the recipe, but to change to lower fat dairy products or even vegetable oils and spreads, e.g. sunflower oil or margarine, where they are not so important. This is the way the recipes in this book have been written.

All the recipes are calorie and fat counted (see *Healthy Living* for guidelines on these) so if you're cutting down on calories and fat it's easy to make your choice.

Follow these tips to help you get the most from your dairy shopping.

Keep a Check on the Date. All pre-packed dairy products are marked with a date guide which states how long the product will keep. This is either in the form of a Sell By date, in which case the label will also say 'Eat within X days of purchase' or a Best Before date which means do not use after that date.

Storing Milk. Heat and light can destroy or affect the flavour of milk so always keep it cool, clean and covered. Only pour out as much as you need in a jug – it keeps better in the bottle or carton. Low fat milk will freeze successfully in the carton.

Treat UHT (long life) and sterilized milk like 'fresh' milk once opened. If you want to keep milk in store buy long-life milk or milk powder as they will keep 3 to 6 months respectively.

Storing Cream. Fresh cream must always be kept in the fridge and used within the 'Sell-by' date. Keep it covered if you don't use the whole pot at once. Treat UHT (long-life) cream as fresh once it's opened. Single cream does not freeze well but if lightly whipped, whipping and double cream will freeze, and, once thawed can be whipped up fully. Thaw cream in the fridge and do not refreeze it.

Storing Butter. It's always best to buy it as fresh as possible and use it within 1-2 weeks. Keep it away from any strong-smelling foods in your fridge to avoid tainting the flavour. Keep butter away from direct sunlight as the vitamins will be quickly destroyed by light, and heat makes it go rancid. Butter can be frozen if well-wrapped. Use it within 3 months.

Storing Cheese. Store for as short a time as possible and always keep well-wrapped and cool to avoid it drying out. The salad drawer in the fridge is a good home for cheese but remember to bring it back to room temperature about an hour before serving to appreciate the flavour. Keep the wraps on till the last moment and then re-wrap leftovers quickly in foil or stretch film.

Frequent changes of temperature may cause soft cheese to go hard and firm cheese to go shiny. If your cheese develops mould on the edges cut the mould off and use the remaining cheese for cooking.

Hard cheeses will freeze up to 3 months but they tend to crumble on thawing so it's best to grate the cheese, keep it in a tub and use it from frozen. Soft and cream cheeses should not be frozen any longer than 1 month or they go hard and yellow.

WHAT ARE DAIRY PRODUCTS?

All dairy products, except eggs (which are not strictly a dairy product), are based on milk, whether it is cow's, sheep's or goat's. Milk has always been regarded as a valuable food because it is a good source of protein. It also provides calcium, and vitamins A, D and B2, which are the nutrients we need to ensure strong healthy bones and teeth. This is particularly important for growing children.

Dairy products have traditionally been regarded as a good source of energy because of the fat they contain. For today's style of healthy living it is a good idea to be aware of the amount of fat in dairy products: and products such as low-fat cheeses and low-fat yoghurt have been developed to help you control the amount of fat in your diet.

The symbols used in the glossary below show the amount of fat in an average daily serving of these products: milk 1 pt (600 ml); smatana and cream 2 tablespoons; yoghurt one 150 g (5 oz) carton (Greek yoghurt, half one 220 g/8 oz carton); butter 25 g (1 oz). Cheese is shown grouped by fat content in the photograph on page 7.

MILK
Milk is usually sold according to fat content. There are 4 main categories:

Channel Islands milk
(Gold Top, Breakfast milk) 4.8% fat
27 g fat (per pint)
The extra creaminess gives body and flavour to recipes like Potatoes au gratin (p.25) and French fruit tart (p.50).

Whole milk 3.8% fat
22 g fat (per pint)
Used for drinking and cooking. Children under five years old should only be given whole milk, not semi-skimmed or skimmed because they need the energy and vitamins that the fat provides.

Semi-skimmed milk 1.5% fat
11 g fat (per pint)

A popular choice with the healthy minded as it's very acceptable for drinking and cooking.

Skimmed milk 0.1% fat
0.6 g fat (per pint)
This has a much thinner consistency than whole milk but is ideal for slimmers or those on low-fat diets.

Before it is sold milk is usually heat treated to make sure it is safe and will keep for a reasonable length of time. The most commonly available types are pasteurized, UHT (longlife cartons) and sterilized.

Pasteurized: Pasteurization is the most delicate heat process used. It ensures that the milk will keep for up to 5 days but has little effect on the flavour. Pasteurized milk may also be *homogenized* — a process which spreads the cream through the milk so it does not separate out.

Ultra High Temperature (UHT) is the process used to produce 'longlife' milk (in cartons). The process sterilizes milk so it will keep unopened for several months without refrigeration but results in only a small loss of flavour. UHT milk has a slightly cooked taste.

Sterilized: Sterilization involves less heat than UHT but over a longer time. This gentle cooking caramalizes the milk sugar and gives sterilized milk its characteristic cooked taste. Unopened this milk will last for several months without refrigeration.

Fermented milk 10% fat
3 g fat (per 2 tablespoons)
This is whole milk to which a special culture has been added. It is pleasantly thick with a milder tang than yoghurt. It's available in this country as Smatana.

YOGHURT
Yoghurt is milk which has been warmed and had a special culture added to it. This causes it to 'set' and gives it its sharp, tangy flavour.

● Cheese is infinitely versatile. It can be eaten at any meal and used in desserts (e.g. the low fat ideas, bottom) and dinner party starters (e.g. baked Bavarian brie, top) as well as main meals, snacks and on its own.

Yoghurt comes flavoured and unflavoured as:

Low-fat yoghurt 1% fat
1.5 g fat (per 150g/5 oz carton)

Thick and creamy yoghurt
3% fat 4.5 g fat (per 150 g/5 oz carton)

Greek yoghurt 10% fat
11.5 g (per 110 g/4 oz serving – half a 220 g carton)

CREAM

Cream has the ability to transform a simple dish – sweet or savoury – into something very special. It is made from milk by a process of separation and is again sold according to different fat content.

Half, single, whipping and double cream can be UHT processed so that it keeps in the pot or carton for 6-8 weeks without refrigeration. Very handy for emergencies.

Half cream 12% fat
3.6 g fat (per 2 tablespoons)
Virtually the same as top of the milk it's particularly good in coffee and can be used in some cooking, see Cucumber and tomato ring (p.16).

Single cream 18% fat
5.7 g fat (per 2 tablespoons)
Mainly used as pouring cream and for sauces, e.g. Pasta with ham and peas (p.33).

Soured cream 18% fat
5.7 g fat (per 2 tablespoons)
Single cream which has had special culture added to it which gives it its pleasant sharp flavour and thicker consistency. Because of its consistency it can be a good lower fat substitute for double cream, for example in Scandinavian herrings (p.14) and Pork with green peppercorn sauce (p.33).

Whipping cream 35-40% fat
11.7 g fat (per 2 tablespoons)

It takes a little longer to whip than double cream but more air is incorporated so it whips up to twice its volume and is very economical for trifles and gâteaux – see Strawberry gâteau (p.51) and Soufflé grand marnier (p.54).

'Thick' or 'extra thick' cream – is specially treated homogenized cream for spooning from the carton. It does not whip and is usually around 35% fat.

Double cream 48% fat
14 g fat (per 2 tablespoons)
Used for everything from Irish coffee (p.60) to Steak au poivre (p.46). It is a good choice for whipping and decorating desserts and gâteaux because with a butterfat content of 48% it holds its shape very well. Add some single cream to the double to make it go further and give a really smooth shine and texture to piping.

Clotted cream 55% fat
19 g fat (per 2 tablespoons)
The most delicious of the creams. It's made by heating pasteurized cream over boiling water for about an hour, then leaving it to chill and set; rich, golden and buttery it is the traditional 'Topper' for scones and jam, or warm mince pies.

Aerosol cream – is UHT cream in aerosol cans. It will keep for 6-8 weeks in the fridge even after opening. You can use as much as you want immediately, with no waste at all. It contains less than half the fat of whipped whipping cream and is usually slightly sweetened.

Frozen cream – commercially frozen single, whipping, double and clotted cream is available in pots or individual portions.

Sterilized cream – made in the same way as sterilized milk, it has a fat content of 23% (or 12% if made from half cream), is sold in cans and will keep virtually indefinitely.

BUTTER 80% fat
20 g fat (per 25 g/1 oz)
Butter is a natural product made from churning cream. The excess liquid (buttermilk) is run off leaving pure butter which naturally contains vitamins A, D and E.

There are basically two types of butter; 'sweet cream' butter is made from pasteurized cream that has been warmed then cooled before churning. It is a golden colour with a rich creamy flavour. 'Lactic' butter is made from cream that has been kept warm after the addition of lactic bacteria. It tends to be light-coloured and sharp-flavoured. Most Dutch and Danish butters are lactic whilst English, Irish and New Zealand butter is generally sweet cream. Unsalted varieties of lactic and sweet cream butter are also available.

Both lactic and sweet cream butter have the same fat content as margarine which is 80%.

DAIRY FULL-FAT SPREADS
70-75% fat 18 g fat (per 25 g/1 oz)
These were developed to be butter substitutes – imitating the taste of butter whilst being easy to spread. They are blends of dairy and/or non-dairy products – for example buttermilk and oil, or cream with oil.

DAIRY LOW-FAT SPREADS
40% fat 10g fat (per 25 g/1 oz)
Made of vegetable oils (40%) with various dairy ingredients to give a butter flavour – buttermilk and butteroil. Primarily for spreading they have limited use in cooking but suit those on a low-fat diet.

CHEESE
Cheese-making is one of the oldest ways of preserving and concentrating fresh whole milk. It takes 8 pints of milk to make a pound of cheese.

There is no easy method for classifying cheeses by appearance or taste. One way might be

1. **Everyday cheeses** – like Cheddar and Cheshire.

2. **Cooking cheeses** – like Mozzarella, Gouda, Emmental, grated cheeses.
3. **Gastronomic cheeses** – Port Salut, Roulé, Brie, Camembert, Stilton.
4. **Fresh cheeses** – these are eaten as soon as they are made – with no pressing. Shelf-life is quite short. For example curd cheese, Quark, Petit Suisse, Ricotta, cream cheese, Fromage Frais. (Fromage frais – or fromage blanc – is a French low fat soft cheese, often sold fruit-flavoured as a dessert and popular as a yoghurt substitute. It can be as low as 1% fat.)
5. **Goat's and sheep's** milk cheeses – and others made from non-cow's milk.
6. **Other cheeses** – cheeses devised for today's healthy living and special diets – low fat cheese and vegetarian cheeses. (Vegetarian cheeses are made without animal rennet. They have the same fat content as the equivalent non vegetarian cheese.)

Another classification can be by fat content (see picture right) though this is not universally recognized. Group 1 are higher fat cheeses – between 20-35% total fat. Included in this category are hard cheeses, some of the blue cheeses including blue brie and full fat cream cheese. These cheeses are all over 100 Calories per 25 g (1 oz).

Group 2 are the medium fat cheeses containing 15-20% total fat, including the half-fat cheeses new to the market as well as cheeses such as mozzarella and feta. These cheeses have between 60-100 Calories per 25 g (1 oz).

Group 3 category includes the lower fat fresh, not-pressed, cheeses, including cottage cheese, curd cheese and ricotta (whey cheese). Total fat in these cheeses is less than 10% so calorific value is under 60 Calories per 25 g (1 oz).

SOUPS AND STARTERS

Watercress and almond soup

Adding ground almonds rather than cream to this soup gives it a delicate nutty flavour and a smooth rich texture.

SERVES 4
750 Kj (180 Calories) per portion
13 g fat per portion

25 g (1 oz) butter
1 onion, chopped
2 bunches watercress, chopped
600 ml (1 pint) vegetable stock
1 tbls cornflour
300 ml (½ pint) semi-skimmed milk
50 g (2 oz) ground almonds
salt and pepper
flaked almonds, toasted, to garnish

Melt the butter in a medium saucepan over a low heat. Add the onion and cook for 3-4 minutes until soft but not browned. Add the watercress and cook for 2 minutes. Stir in the stock. Cover the pan and simmer for 10 minutes.

Transfer the soup to a blender or food processor. Blend until smooth. Return the soup to the pan.

Blend the cornflour in a small bowl with a tablespoon of the milk to make a smooth, creamy paste. Add the paste to the soup. Stir in the rest of the milk and the ground almonds. Season to taste. Place the pan over a moderate heat for 5 minutes to re-heat the soup, stirring all the time.

Serve in individual bowls with a few toasted flaked almonds sprinkled over.

Blue cheese and onion soup

SERVES 4
710 Kj (170 Calories) per portion
10 g fat per portion

25 g (1 oz) butter or margarine
1 large onion, finely chopped
25 g (1 oz) plain flour
450 ml (¾ pint) chicken stock
300 ml (½ pint) skimmed milk
75 g (3 oz) Danish blue or blue Brie cheese, rind removed
salt and pepper
snipped chives, to garnish

Melt the butter or margarine in a saucepan over a low heat. Add the onion and cook gently until the onion is soft but not browned. Stir in the flour. Gradually stir in the chicken stock and the milk. Increase the heat and bring the liquid to the boil, stirring all the time.

Cut the cheese into small pieces and add them to the soup. Reduce the heat and stir until the cheese has melted.

Gently reheat the soup and season to taste. Serve in individual bowls sprinkled with snipped chives.

Serving idea: Serve with a savoury bread, for example onion-flavoured bread, or a multi-grained rye bread.

● **Watercress and almond soup;**
Blue cheese and onion soup

Sweetcorn and crab chowder

SERVES 4

710 Kj (170 Calories) per portion
8 g fat per portion

25 g (1 oz) butter or margarine
1 onion, chopped
2 tbls plain flour
450 ml (¾ pint) chicken stock
450 ml (¾ pint) semi-skimmed
    milk
175 g (6 oz) frozen sweetcorn
    kernels
2 tbls dry sherry
100 g (4 oz) crabsticks, chopped
    and flaked
salt and pepper
chopped parsley, to garnish

Melt the butter or margarine in a large saucepan over a low heat. Add the onion and cook gently for 4-5 minutes until soft but not browned.

Stir in the flour. Gradually blend in the stock and milk.

Put 50 g (2 oz) of the sweetcorn to one side. Add the remainder to the pan with the sherry. Increase the heat and bring the liquid to the boil. Reduce the heat and simmer for 15 minutes.

Working in two batches, pour the soup into a blender or food processor. Blend briefly, still retaining some of the texture of the sweetcorn. Stir in the crabsticks and reserved sweetcorn. Season to taste and return the soup to the saucepan. Place the pan over a moderate heat for 4-5 minutes to heat the soup through.

Serve immediately, sprinkled with chopped parsley.

Serving idea: Serve with crusty bread or wholemeal rolls.

Variations: Use fresh white crabmeat if available.

Salmon mousse

SERVES 4
610 Kj (145 Calories) per portion
8 g fat per portion

150 ml (¼ pint) vegetable stock
15 g (½ oz) sachet powdered
gelatine
220 g (7½ oz) can medium red
salmon, drained
1 tbls lemon juice
1 tsp tomato purée
150 ml (¼ pint) creamed smatana
or fromage frais
½ tsp chopped fresh tarragon
1 egg, separated
salt and pepper
To garnish
lemon slices
parsley

Place the vegetable stock in a small bowl and sprinkle the gelatine on top. Leave for a few minutes until it is spongy. Set the bowl in a saucepan of hot water and stir until the gelatine has dissolved.

Remove all the bones and skin from the salmon. Put the flesh into a blender or food processor with the lemon juice, tomato purée, smatana, tarragon, and egg yolk. Purée several times until smooth. Add the dissolved gelatine and season to taste. Transfer the mixture to a bowl. Whisk the egg white until it forms stiff peaks, and fold it into the mixture.

Rinse a 600 ml (1 pint) fish mould with cold water. Pour in the fish mousse, smoothing the surface with a palette knife. Leave it in the refrigerator to set. Turn the mousse out on to a flat dish. To serve, garnish with lemon slices and sprigs of parsley.

Serving idea: Serve with wholemeal bread or melba toast.

Variation: Try using tuna fish if preferred. If a fish mould is not available set the mousse in a bowl, soufflé dish, or individual dishes, and do not turn it out.

Smoked mackerel mousse

SERVES 4
500 Kj (120 Calories) per portion
8 g fat per portion

150 g (5 oz) smoked mackerel fillets
113 g (4 oz) carton cottage cheese
1 tbls natural yoghurt
1 tsp creamed horseradish
black pepper
parsley sprigs, to garnish

Remove all the skin and any large bones from the fillets. If using a food processor, it should mince any tiny bones. Place all the ingredients in a food processor or blender and blend until they are thoroughly combined and completely smooth. Check the seasoning, adding a little more horseradish if necessary.

Transfer to a deep dish and garnish with the parsley before serving.

Serving idea: Serve with hot toast or fingers of pitta bread. Alternatively serve in individual ramekins, with cucumber slices and crudités. Hand a sweet and sour dressing separately.

Variation: Use smoked trout instead, for a delicious and light flavoured mousse.

• Sweetcorn and crab chowder; Smoked mackerel mousse; Salmon mousse

Scandinavian herrings

SERVES 4
1110 Kj (265 Calories) per portion
19 g fat per portion

350 g (12 oz) jar herring fillets or
*   3 rollmop herrings*
4 spring onions, chopped
1 red dessert apple, cored and
*   chopped*
50 g (2 oz) sweet and sour
*   gherkins, chopped*
1 tbls lemon juice
142 ml (5 fl oz) carton soured cream
2 tbls chopped fresh dill

Drain the herrings and cut them into 2.5 cm (1 inch) pieces. Put them into a bowl with the spring onions, apple and gherkins. In a small bowl, mix the lemon juice, cream and 1 tablespoon of dill. Stir this dressing into the herring mixture.

Turn the salad into a serving dish and scatter the rest of the chopped dill on top.

Serving idea: Serve with dark rye bread or pumpernickel.

Egg and prawn soufflés

SERVES 4
710 Kj (170 Calories) per portion
13 g fat per portion

3 hard-boiled eggs, finely chopped
100 g (4 oz) peeled prawns,
*   chopped*
2 spring onions, finely chopped
2 tbls mayonnaise
3 tbls soured cream
4 drops Tabasco sauce or ½ tsp
*   anchovy essence*
2 tsp powdered gelatine
salt and pepper
1 egg white
To garnish
1 hard-boiled egg, finely chopped
4 anchovy fillets

Put the chopped eggs, prawns and spring onions into a bowl and mix well. Blend the mayonnaise, soured cream and the Tabasco sauce together. Sprinkle the gelatine on to 3 tbls water in a small bowl. Leave for a few minutes until it is spongy. Set the bowl in a saucepan of hot water and stir until the gelatine has dissolved. Cool slightly. Whisk into the mayonnaise mixture. Fold the mayonnaise into the egg mixture and season to taste. Chill in the refrigerator until it is just beginning to thicken.

Whisk the egg white until it forms stiff peaks and fold it into the soufflé mixture. Turn it into 4 individual ramekin dishes and refrigerate until set.

To serve, garnish each soufflé with chopped egg and an anchovy fillet.

Serving idea: Make double quantities in a large soufflé dish and serve with a salad, for a light lunch.

Courgettes with tzatziki

SERVES 4
1045 Kj (250 Calories) per portion
12 g fat per portion

4 firm courgettes
1 egg, beaten
salt and pepper
40 g (1½ oz) wholemeal flour
vegetable oil for shallow frying
For the tzatziki
½ cucumber, peeled and finely
  chopped
2 × 150 g (5.29 oz) cartons natural
  yoghurt
1 small clove garlic, crushed
1 tbls olive oil
1 tsp wine vinegar
1 tsp dill seeds
cucumber slices, to garnish

Make the tzatziki first. In a mixing bowl, combine the cucumber with the yoghurt, garlic, oil, vinegar and dill seeds. Mix well and place the

• Scandinavian herrings;
Egg and prawn soufflés;
Courgettes with tzatziki

mixture in the refrigerator.

Top and tail the courgettes. Wipe them on damp kitchen paper. Cut each one lengthways into 4 even strips. Dip each one into beaten egg and coat completely in seasoned flour. Heat the oil in a frying pan over a high heat. Fry the courgette slices briskly for 2 minutes on each side. When they are golden brown all over, lift them on to absorbent kitchen paper. Transfer to a warm serving dish and serve immediately with the chilled and garnished tzatziki.

Variation: Use thinly sliced aubergine, instead of courgettes, and fry on each side for about 5 minutes.

VEGETABLE MAIN MEALS AND ACCOMPANIMENTS

Cucumber and tomato ring

SERVES 4

880 Kj (210 Calories) per portion

7 g fat per portion

2 × 397 g (14 oz) cans tomatoes
½ onion, chopped
2 cloves garlic, crushed
1 small carrot, chopped
50 ml (2 fl oz) red wine or port
2 tsp brown sugar
Tabasco sauce to taste
2 cloves
1 bay leaf
strip of lemon rind
15 g (½ oz) sachet powdered
   gelatine
150 g (5.29 oz) carton natural
   yoghurt
1 tbls fresh, chopped parsley and/or
   basil
1 bunch watercress, to garnish

For the cucumber layer

15 g (½ oz) sachet powdered
   gelatine
1 cucumber, peeled and chopped
225 g (8 oz) skimmed milk cheese
2 tbls white wine vinegar
½ tsp dried tarragon
½ tsp caster sugar
142 ml (5 fl oz) half cream
1 tbls fresh mint, chopped
   (optional)

First prepare the tomato mixture. Place the tomatoes with their juice, the onion, garlic, carrot, wine, sugar, Tabasco, cloves, bay leaf and lemon rind in a large saucepan. Combine well. Bring to the boil and simmer over a moderate heat for 20 minutes. Allow to cool. Soak the gelatine in 5 tbls cold water in a small heatproof bowl and set aside. Strain the tomato mixture into a mixing bowl; there should be about 300 ml

(½ pint). Blend in the yoghurt. Place the bowl with the gelatine in a pan of simmering water and stir until dissolved. Very carefully add it to the mixture with the herbs. Stir occasionally while the cucumber mixture is being prepared.

To prepare the cucumber layer, soak the gelatine in 5 tbls cold water in a small heatproof bowl and set aside. Mix the cucumber with the cheese, vinegar, tarragon, sugar, cream and mint. Dissolve the gelatine as above and blend very thoroughly into the cucumber mixture.

Transfer the tomato mixture to a metal bowl or saucepan so that it will get cold quickly. When the mixture begins to thicken pour it into a

1.2 litre (2 pint) ring mould, lightly brushed with olive oil. Chill in the refrigerator until it is firm enough to support the cucumber mixture, about 30 minutes. When firm, spoon the cucumber evenly over it. Cover with clingfilm and chill for 2 hours, or until firm.

To turn out the mousse, loosen the jelly all the way round gently with a knife. Put a plate over the top, and invert the mould on to the plate. Fill the centre of the ring with a bouquet of watercress and serve at room temperature.

Serving idea: Serve with hot bread flavoured with garlic, herbs or anchovies, and fill the centre of the ring with tomato and watercress.

Variation: Make up the mixtures in individual ramekins if wished.

● Cucumber and tomato ring with individual variations

Vegetable quiche

SERVES 6
2010 Kj (480 Calories) per portion
31 g fat per portion

150 g (5 oz) wholemeal flour
50 g (2 oz) oatmeal
75 g (3 oz) butter or margarine
25 g (1 oz) white polyunsaturated
  fat
1 egg yolk mixed with 3 tbls cold
  water
For the filling
40 g (1 ½ oz) butter
3 medium carrots, sliced
2 medium onions, sliced
2 medium parsnips, sliced
450 g (1 lb) fresh spinach, trimmed
  and washed, or 225 g (8 oz)
  frozen spinach defrosted
For the sauce
300 ml (½ pint) semi-skimmed
  milk
1 bay leaf
slice of onion and carrot
15 g (½ oz) butter or margarine
15 g (½ oz) plain flour
2 eggs, size 2
100 g (4 oz) Gruyère cheese,
  grated

Prepare the milk for the sauce by heating it gently without boiling with the bay leaf, onion and carrot. Set aside.

To make the pastry, sift the flour into a mixing bowl and discard the bran from the sieve. Add the oatmeal and rub in the fats. Work the mixture with your fingertips until it resembles fine breadcrumbs. Mix in the egg and water, adding more cold water if necessary, to make a firm dough. Knead lightly on a floured board and roll out to line a 20 cm (8 inch) deep flan ring or dish.

Heat the oven to 190°C, 375°F, Gas Mark 5. If using a ceramic dish, line the pastry with greaseproof paper, and fill with baking beans and bake in the oven for 10 minutes to set the pastry. Remove the paper and beans.

Meanwhile, prepare the filling. Melt the butter in a frying pan over a moderate heat. Cook the vegetables, except the spinach, until they are soft. Set aside to cool. Place the spinach in a medium saucepan. Cover and cook over a moderately high heat for about 5 minutes. Press the leaves between 2 plates to remove all excess moisture, and chop them roughly. Leave the spinach to cool while preparing the sauce.

Melt the butter or margarine in a small saucepan over a moderate heat. Blend in the flour, and cook for 1 minute. Strain the milk and gradually pour it into the pan, stirring constantly. Bring the sauce to the boil, still stirring.

When the sauce has thickened, remove the pan from the heat and whisk the sauce for 1 minute to cool it down. Beat in the eggs one at a time. Add half the grated cheese. Season to taste.

Spread the spinach over the bottom of the flan. Cover it evenly with the mixed vegetables, and carefully spoon the sauce on top. Sprinkle with the rest of the cheese and bake in the oven for about 45 minutes until golden brown and crisp. Allow to stand with the oven turned off for 10 minutes before placing on a cooling rack.

Serving idea: Serve warm or cold with baked or new potatoes and a mixed salad.

Variation: Try leeks and/or salsify instead of the carrots or parsnips.

● Vegetable quiche; Fisherman's potatoes

Fisherman's potatoes

SERVES 4
1550 Kj (370 Calories) per portion
9 g fat per portion

4 medium potatoes
350 g (12 oz) smoked haddock
150 ml (¼ pint) skimmed milk
142 ml (5 fl oz) carton soured cream
2 tbls chopped dill or fresh chives
salt and pepper

Heat the oven to 200°C, 400°F, Gas Mark 6.

Scrub the potatoes and prick them with a fork. Place in the oven and cook for about 1 hour until they are tender when squeezed.

Meanwhile, place the fish in an ovenproof dish. Pour over the milk. Cover the dish and cook in the oven for 15 minutes or until the fish flesh flakes when prodded with a fork. Drain the fish, discarding the milk. Remove the skin and place the fish in a saucepan. Mix in the soured cream and dill. Season the mixture to taste. Set the pan over a low heat and gently warm the fish through without boiling.

Cut a cross in the top of each cooked potato and squeeze gently to open them up a little. Spoon over the fish topping. Serve immediately.

Serving idea: Serve with coleslaw or a mixed salad.

Variation: To save time, use smoked mackerel fillets which do not need prior cooking.

Sesame and tuna quiche

SERVES 6

1510 Kj (360 Calories) per portion
20 g fat per portion

2 tbls sesame seeds, lightly toasted
175 g (6 oz) plain flour, sifted
pinch salt
40 g (1½ oz) butter or margarine
40 g (1½ oz) white
    polyunsaturated fat
For the filling
198 g (7 oz) can tuna in brine,
    drained
225 g (8 oz) frozen sweetcorn
    kernels, thawed
½ bunch spring onions, trimmed
    and chopped
3 eggs
150 g (5.29 oz) carton natural
    yoghurt
pepper
50 g (2 oz) Double Gloucester
    cheese, finely grated

Heat the oven to 200°C, 400°F, Gas Mark 6.

Combine the sesame seeds with the flour and salt in a mixing bowl. Add the margarine and fat and rub them in until the mixture resembles fine breadcrumbs. Add 4-5 tbls chilled water and mix to a dough. Knead the dough briefly.

Roll out the pastry on a floured surface and use it to line a 23 cm (9 inch) flan tin. Prick the pastry all over with a fork. Line it with foil or greaseproof paper and baking beans. Bake in the oven for 12 minutes. Remove the foil and beans. Reduce the temperature to 190°C, 375°F, Gas Mark 5. Bake the pastry case for a further 10 minutes or until it is cooked through and golden. Set aside.

Put the tuna into a bowl and break it up with a fork. Mix in the sweetcorn and spring onion. In a separate bowl, beat together the eggs and yoghurt. Season with pepper. Pour on to the tuna mixture and mix well.

Spoon the mixture into the pastry case. Scatter the cheese on top and bake in the oven for 25-30 minutes until the filling is set and golden.

Serving idea: Serve hot with new potatoes and a green vegetable, or cold with salad.

Variation: Use pink salmon instead of tuna and sprinkle extra sesame seeds on top if liked.

Greek salad

As Feta cheese tends to be salty, soak it in water to give it a milder flavour.

SERVES 4

1045 Kj (250 Calories) per portion
22 g fat per portion

225 g (8 oz) young spinach leaves
½ cucumber, cut into chunks
½ bunch radishes, halved
½ Spanish onion, thinly sliced
175 g (6 oz) Feta cheese, soaked in
    cold water for 20 minutes
12 black olives
For the dressing
3 tbls olive oil
1 tbls red wine vinegar
1 tbls mixed fresh herbs e.g. chives,
    marjoram and parsley
salt and pepper

Wash the spinach leaves. Trim off the stalks and tear the larger leaves into smaller pieces. Dry the spinach well and put into a salad bowl with the cucumber, radishes, and onion.

To make the dressing, place all the ingredients in a clean screw-top jar and shake well. Pour over the salad and toss together. Drain the cheese and dry it well on absorbent kitchen paper. Cut it into small cubes and add to the salad. Garnish with the black olives and serve immediately.

Serving idea: Serve with crusty bread and Greek or Spanish wine.

• Sesame and tuna quiche; Greek salad

Golden vegetable loaf

SERVES 4-6
1045 Kj (250 Calories) per portion
13 g fat per portion

1 tbls oil
225 g (8 oz) carrots, grated
350 g (12 oz) swede, grated
175 g (6 oz) courgettes, grated
225 g (8 oz) leeks, shredded
100 g (4 oz) wholemeal
  breadcrumbs
100 g (4 oz) half-fat Cheddar
  cheese, grated
3 eggs, beaten
3 tbls natural yoghurt
1 tbls chopped parsley
salt and pepper

Lightly grease a 1 kg (2 lb) loaf tin. Heat the oven to 190°C, 375°F, Gas Mark 5.

Put the oil into a large saucepan set over a low heat. Add all the vegetables, cover the pan and gently sweat them for 10 minutes. Away from the heat stir in the remaining ingredients and mix well. Turn the vegetable mixture into the prepared tin, smooth over the top and bake in the oven for 45 minutes until firm. Leave the loaf to stand in the tin for 5 minutes before turning it out on to a serving plate.

When serving, cut into slices with a very sharp knife, supporting each piece with a fish slice.

Serving idea: Serve hot with small new potatoes, or cold with a tomato salad. Reheated leftovers also make an excellent vegetable side dish for meat or poultry.

● Vegetable and egg curry; Parsnip and cheese souffle; Golden vegetable loaf

Vegetable and egg curry

SERVES 4
1090 Kj (260 Calories) per portion
17 g fat per portion

225 g (8 oz) aubergine, diced
salt
2 tbls oil
1 onion, chopped
1 clove garlic, crushed
2 tbls concentrated curry paste
1 small cauliflower, cut into florets
225 g (8 oz) courgettes, thickly
   sliced
397 g (14 oz) can tomatoes
150 g (5.29 oz) carton smatana or
   natural yoghurt
salt and pepper
6 hard-boiled eggs
chopped coriander, to garnish

Sprinkle the aubergine with salt and leave to stand for 30 minutes. Rinse well, drain and dry on absorbent kitchen paper.

Heat the oil in a large frying pan over a medium heat. Add the aubergine, onion and garlic and cook for 5 minutes. Stir in the curry paste. Add the cauliflower, courgettes and tomatoes roughly chopped, with their juice. Gradually blend in the smatana. Season to taste, cover the pan and simmer for 20 minutes.

In the meantime shell the eggs. When the vegetables are tender, spoon them into a warmed serving dish and pour over all the sauce. Quarter the eggs and arrange them on top. Sprinkle with coriander and serve.

Serving idea: Serve with brown rice, and garnish with crisply fried onion rings or chopped spring onions.

Note: If you do not have any curry paste, use 2 tbls Madras Curry powder mixed with 1 tbls boiling water and add in the same way.

Parsnip and cheese soufflé

SERVES 4-6
1590 Kj (380 Calories) per portion
24 g fat per portion

450 g (1 lb) parsnips, roughly
   chopped
knob of butter
1 tbls breadcrumbs
1 tbls grated Parmesan cheese
25 g (1 oz) sunflower margarine
40 g (1½ oz) wholemeal flour
300 ml (½ pint) semi-skimmed
   milk
3 egg yolks
100 g (4 oz) vegetarian cheese,
   grated
2 tbls chopped parsley
salt and pepper
pinch of cayenne pepper
4 egg whites

Grease a 1.75 litre (3 pint) soufflé dish with the butter. Coat with the breadcrumbs and Parmesan. Heat the oven to 220°C, 425°F, Gas Mark 7.

Place the parsnips in a saucepan and just cover with lightly salted water. Bring to the boil and cook until tender. Drain, and either mash them or blend in a food processor to make a purée. Set aside.

Melt the margarine in a small saucepan over a low heat. Stir in the flour and cook for 1 minute. Gradually add the milk, stirring all the time. Simmer for 2 minutes.

Remove the pan from heat and beat in the egg yolks one at a time. Stir in the parsnip purée, grated cheese and parsley. Add seasoning.

Whisk the egg whites in a bowl until they form stiff peaks. Beat 2 tablespoons into the parsnip mixture and carefully fold in the rest. Turn the soufflé mixture into the prepared dish and cook in the oven for 15 minutes. Reduce the heat to 200°C, 400°F, Gas Mark 6 and continue to cook a further 20 minutes. Serve immediately.

Cucumber and mint cheesecake

SERVES 6
1300 Kj (310 Calories) per portion
19 g fat per portion

75 g (3 oz) butter or margarine
175 g (6 oz) wholemeal bran
  biscuits, crushed
15 g (½ oz) sachet powdered
  gelatine
225 g (8 oz) low-fat soft cheese
225 g (8 oz) cottage cheese, sieved
1 egg, separated
½ cucumber, peeled and finely
  diced
1 tbls chopped mint
pinch garlic salt
To garnish
cucumber slices
sprigs of mint

Melt the butter in a small pan and pour it over the crushed biscuits, in a bowl. Mix well and spoon into the base of a 20 cm (8 inch) loose-bottomed or spring-form tin. Press the crumbs down evenly and set the tin aside.

Sprinkle the gelatine over 3 tbls water in a bowl. Set the bowl over a pan of hot water and stir until the gelatine has dissolved.

In a clean mixing bowl, beat the cheeses with the egg yolk until smooth. Fold in the gelatine, cucumber and mint and season with garlic salt.

Whisk the egg white until it forms stiff peaks and fold it into the cheese mixture. Pour the mixture into the tin, spreading it evenly over the biscuit base. Chill in the refrigerator until set.

When the cheesecake is set, remove it from the tin. Garnish with cucumber slices and sprigs of mint.

● **Cucumber and mint cheesecake;**
Nutty lentil bake;
Potatoes au gratin

Nutty lentil bake

SERVES 4-6
2090 Kj (500 Calories) per portion
22 g fat per portion

350 g (12 oz) red lentils, rinsed
2 bay leaves
25 g (1 oz) butter
1 onion, chopped
2 sticks celery, finely sliced
75 g (3 oz) Brazil nuts, roughly
  chopped
1 tsp coriander seeds, crushed
1 tbls chopped parsley
100 g (4 oz) low-fat Cheddar
  cheese, grated
salt and pepper
25 g (1 oz) wholemeal
  breadcrumbs

Put the lentils into a saucepan with 900 ml (1½ pints) water and the bay leaves. Bring to the boil. Reduce the heat and simmer for 45 minutes, beating to a thick paste towards the end.

Heat the oven to 200°C, 400°F, Gas Mark 6.

While the lentils are cooking, melt

the butter in a saucepan over a low heat. Add the onion and celery and cook for 3-4 minutes until they are soft. Mix into the lentils with 50 g (2 oz) of the nuts, the coriander seeds, parsley and 75 g (3 oz) of the cheese. Season to taste and spoon into a large greased ovenproof dish.

Combine the remaining nuts and cheese with the breadcrumbs. Scatter over the top of the dish and bake in the oven for 30 minutes until golden. Serve hot.

Serving idea: Serve with a tomato salad or spring greens.

Variation: Use peanuts instead of Brazil nuts, or omit nuts and use 100 g (4 oz) chopped mushrooms.

Potatoes au gratin

Breakfast milk is Channel Islands milk which has been treated so that the fat is evenly distributed throughout. While rich and creamy, it is lower in fat than the single cream which is customarily used.

SERVES 4
920 Kj (220 Calories) per portion
7 g fat per portion

750 g (1 ½ lb) potatoes, thinly sliced
1 clove garlic, crushed
15 g (½ oz) butter
pinch of nutmeg
125 ml (4 fl oz) Breakfast (Jersey) milk
40 g (1 ½ oz) Gruyère cheese, finely grated

Heat the oven to 180°C, 350°F, Gas Mark 4. Put the potato slices into a saucepan and cover with cold water. Bring to the boil and cook for 2 minutes. Drain well.

Mix the garlic in a small bowl with the butter. Use the butter to grease the inside of an ovenproof dish. Arrange the potato slices in layers.

Mix the nutmeg and milk together and pour over the potatoes. Sprinkle the cheese on top and cook in the oven for 45 minutes until golden.

Serving idea: Serve hot as an accompaniment to roast or grilled meats.

Vegetable casserole with cheese scones

SERVES 4 as a main meal
1860 Kj (445 Calories) per portion
21 g fat per portion

1 tbls oil
1 onion, chopped
225 g (8 oz) white turnips, diced
225 g (8 oz) carrots, sliced
350 g (12 oz) leeks, chopped
225 g (8 oz) courgettes, sliced
397 g (14 oz) can tomatoes
1 tbls tomato purée
150 ml (¼ pint) vegetable stock
1 tsp mixed herbs
salt and pepper
For the scones
50 g (2 oz) margarine
1 small onion, finely chopped
225 g (8 oz) self-raising flour
pinch of salt
75 g (3 oz) Double Gloucester
   cheese with onions and chives,
   finely grated
4-5 tbls skimmed milk

Heat the oven to 200°C, 400°F, Gas Mark 6.

Put the oil into a large saucepan over a moderate heat. Add the onion, turnips, carrots and leeks. Cover and cook for 10 minutes. Stir in the courgettes, the tomatoes with their juice, the tomato purée and stock. Raise the heat and bring to the boil. Simmer for 5 minutes. Stir in the herbs, season to taste, and transfer to an ovenproof casserole.

To make the scones, melt 15 g (½ oz) of the margarine in a saucepan. Add the onion and cook for 4 minutes until soft. Leave to cool.

In a mixing bowl, rub the remaining margarine into the flour with the salt. Stir in the onion and the cheese. Add the milk and mix to a soft dough. Knead lightly on a floured surface. Roll the dough out to a thickness of 2 cm (¾ inch) and cut out rounds 5 cm (2 inches) in diameter. Place the scones on top of the vegetables, brush with a little milk and cook in the oven for 20-25 minutes until the scones are golden. Serve immediately.

Serving idea: This dish makes a complete vegetarian meal or may be served as an accompaniment to grilled lamb chops.

Variation: Use other vegetables of your choice such as parsnips, swede, mushrooms and celery, and try Sage Derby or Red Leicester cheese with the scones.

Risotto milanese

SERVES 4
1880 Kj (450 Calories) per portion
12 g fat per portion

1 tbls olive oil
1 small onion, chopped
350 g (12 oz) brown rice
pinch of saffron
85 ml (3 fl oz) dry white wine
750 ml (1¼ pints) hot chicken stock
salt and pepper
100 g (4 oz) Dolcelatte cheese
15 g (½ oz) grated Parmesan
   cheese

Heat the oil in a large saucepan over a gentle heat. Add the onion and cook for 4 minutes until soft but not browned. Add the rice and stir until all the grains are coated with oil. Stir the saffron into the wine and add it to the rice. Let it sizzle for a few moments and pour in the stock. Reduce the heat to low, cover the pan and leave the rice to cook for 30 minutes. Towards the end of the cooking time, check that it is not sticking to the bottom of the pan; if it is, add a little water.

When the rice is tender, season to taste. Cut the Dolcelatte cheese into small pieces and stir them into the rice. Turn the risotto into a warm serving dish and sprinkle the Parmesan cheese on top. Serve.

Serving idea: This is a good dish to have on its own or as an accompaniment to grilled meats.

• Vegetable casserole with cheese scones; Risotto milanese; Stuffed tomatoes

Stuffed tomatoes

SERVES 4
710 Kj (170 Calories) per portion
10 g fat per portion

4 large tomatoes, each weighing about 225 g (8 oz) or 8 medium tomatoes
salt and pepper
1 tbls oil
1 small onion
50 g (2 oz) bulgur wheat or cooked brown rice
50 g (2 oz) mushrooms, chopped
½ small green pepper, seeded and chopped
1 tsp mixed herbs
dash of Tabasco sauce
75 g (3 oz) Austrian smoked cheese, grated
mint sprigs, to garnish

Heat the oven to 190°C, 375°F, Gas Mark 5.

Slice off the tops of the tomatoes and keep them to one side to be used as lids. Scoop out the seeds and flesh with a teaspoon, taking care not to pierce the skins. Reserve the pulp.

Sprinkle the insides of the tomatoes with a little salt and turn them upside down to drain.

Heat the oil in a medium saucepan over a moderate heat. Add the onion and cook gently for 4 minutes. Add the bulgur wheat or cooked rice and cook, stirring for 1 minute. Stir in 2 tablespoons of the tomato pulp with the mushrooms and chopped pepper and add the herbs and Tabasco sauce. Simmer uncovered for 10 minutes. Stir in the cheese and season to taste.

Spoon the filling into the tomato shells. Replace the lids, and arrange the tomatoes in an ovenproof dish. Cook in the oven for 20 minutes. Garnish and serve while still hot.

Chicken with mushrooms

SERVES 4
2420 Kj (580 Calories) per portion
11 g fat per portion

approx 1.5 kg (3 lb) chicken
  portions, as: 4 drumsticks and 2
  breasts
1 tbls lemon juice
50 ml (2 fl oz) dry sherry
200 g (7 oz) button mushrooms
For the sauce
475 ml (16 fl oz) semi-skimmed
  milk
1 bay leaf
1 clove
1 slice onion
50 g (2 oz) butter or margarine
50 g (2 oz) plain flour
chopped parsley, to garnish

Heat the oven to 190°C, 375°F, Gas Mark 5.

Heat the milk in a small saucepan over a gentle heat with the bay leaf, clove and onion. Remove the pan from the heat before the milk reaches boiling point, and set aside for the flavours to infuse.

Skin the chicken pieces and cut the breast joints into 2. Pack the chicken tightly into a small flameproof casserole. Pour over the lemon juice and sherry. Simmer gently for 5 minutes. Cover first with buttered paper, then the lid, and transfer to the oven. Cook for 40 minutes, or until the juices run clear when the leg is pierced with the point of a sharp knife.

To make the sauce, melt the butter or margarine in a large saucepan over a moderate heat. Stir in the

flour and cook for 1 minute. Strain the milk and add it to the pan. stirring constantly. Bring to the boil, still stirring, and simmer for 2 minutes. Cover the pan and remove from the heat. Remove the chicken from the casserole with a slotted spoon and keep warm and covered.

Strain all the chicken juices into the sauce. Place the pan over a moderate heat and simmer gently for about 10 minutes, until the sauce is rich and creamy.

Wipe the mushrooms. If they are large, cut them into quarters. Add to the sauce and simmer for 5 minutes. Season to taste. Serve the chicken with the sauce spooned over and garnished with the parsley.

Serving idea: Serve with fresh pasta and steamed vegetables.

Chicken noodle gratin

SERVES 4
2240 Kj (535 Calories) per portion
18 g fat per portion

450 g (1 lb) cooked chicken
100 g (4 oz) mushrooms, sliced
salt
225 g (8 oz) tagliatelle
1 tsp sunflower oil
For the tomato sauce
2 tsp sunflower oil
1 small onion, finely chopped
1 clove garlic
397 g (14 oz) can chopped tomatoes
½ tsp dried basil
salt and pepper
For the cheese sauce
25 g (1 oz) butter or margarine
25 g (1 oz) plain flour
300 ml (½ pint) semi-skimmed milk
25 g (1 oz) Parmesan or medium fat hard cheese, grated

Heat the oven to 200°C, 400°F, Gas Mark 6.

Cut the chicken into large pieces and put into a bowl with the mushrooms. Set aside.

Bring a large pan of salted water to the boil. Add the tagliatelle and the oil and boil for 10-12 minutes or until barely tender.

Meanwhile, make the tomato sauce. Heat the oil in a medium saucepan over a moderate heat. Add the onion and garlic and cook for 3-4 minutes until soft but not browned. Stir in the tomatoes and basil. Season to taste and simmer, uncovered, for 10 minutes.

Drain the pasta and place in the bottom of a greased ovenproof dish. Pour the tomato sauce over the pasta.

To make the cheese sauce, melt the butter in a small saucepan over a moderate heat. Stir in the flour and cook for 1 minute. Gradually blend in the milk, stirring constantly, and cook until the sauce is thick. Season to taste. Remove the pan from the heat. Add half of the cheese to the sauce, stirring until it has melted.

Combine half of the cheese sauce with the chicken and mushrooms. Spoon this mixture evenly over the pasta. Cover with the rest of the cheese sauce and sprinkle the remaining cheese on top. Cook in the oven for 25 minutes until lightly golden. Serve immediately.

Serving idea: Serve with a green salad, crusty bread and a robust Italian wine such as Valpolicella or Bardolino.

Variation: Left-over turkey makes a good substitute for the chicken.

● Chicken noodle gratin; Chicken with mushrooms

Chicken in cashew nut sauce

SERVES 4
2100 Kj (500 Calories) per portion
30 g fat per portion

4 chicken portions, cut in half
2 tsp lemon juice
2 tbls sunflower oil
1 onion, finely chopped
1 clove garlic, crushed
1 green pepper, seeded and sliced
½ tsp turmeric
2 tsp ground cumin
3 tsp ground coriander
½ tsp ground cinnamon
½ tsp ground ginger
½ tsp paprika
300 ml (½ pint) chicken stock
150 g (5.29 oz) carton natural
yoghurt
50 g (2 oz) cashew nuts, finely
ground
salt and pepper
To garnish
25 g (1 oz) cashew nuts, toasted
sliced green pepper

Skin the chicken pieces, sprinkle them with the lemon juice and set aside.

In a large flameproof casserole, heat the oil over a moderate heat. Cook the onion for 5 minutes until softened but not browned. Add the garlic and pepper and cook for a further 2 minutes. Add the spices and cook for 1 minute, stirring well. Pour in the stock, still stirring, and add the chicken. Blend in the yoghurt a tablespoonful at a time. Cover the casserole and simmer gently for 30 minutes.

Stir in the ground cashew nuts and season to taste. Replace the cover and continue to cook for 10 minutes.

Serve garnished with the toasted cashew nuts and slices of green pepper.

Serving idea: Serve with either Indian bread or basmati rice and a selection of side dishes such as chopped tomato and onion, Indian pickles or sliced banana.

Stuffed chicken breasts

SERVES 4
1045 Kj (250 Calories) per portion
12 g fat per portion

4 chicken breasts, boned and
skinned
100 g (4 oz) low-fat soft cheese with
herbs and garlic
salt and pepper
15 g (½ oz) butter or margarine
1 tbls sunflower oil
175 g (6 oz) button mushrooms,
thickly sliced
300 ml (½ pint) chicken stock
3 tbls dry white wine
2 tsp cornflour
chopped parsley, to garnish

Make a horizontal incision in each chicken breast to form a pocket. Divide the cheese into 4 equal portions and use it to stuff the chicken breasts. Secure each opening with a cocktail stick. Season the chicken portions.

In a large frying pan over a moderate heat, heat the butter and oil. Cook the chicken for 5-7 minutes on each side until lightly golden. Remove the chicken from the pan and set aside in a warm place. Place the mushrooms in the pan and cook for 3 minutes.

Return the chicken to the pan and pour over the stock and wine. Cover the pan and simmer for 15 minutes.

Blend the cornflour with 1 or 2 teaspoons of water. Pour into the pan and continue to cook over a low heat, stirring all the time until the sauce thickens.

To serve, transfer the chicken portions to a deep serving dish. Remove the cocktail sticks, pour over the sauce and sprinkle chopped parsley on top.

● **Chicken in cashew nut sauce; Stuffed chicken breasts**

● Country rabbit pies; Pasta with ham and peas; Pork with green peppercorn sauce

Country rabbit pies

SERVES 4
2930 Kj (700 Calories) per portion
40 g fat per portion

750 g (1½ lb) diced rabbit,
　defrosted if frozen
25 g (1 oz) butter or margarine
1 onion, chopped
1 tbls plain flour
250 ml (8 fl oz) chicken stock
1 tsp grated lemon rind
juice of ½ lemon
2 carrots, thinly sliced
½ tsp dried mixed herbs
100 g (4 oz) button mushrooms,
　halved
142 ml (5 fl oz) single cream
salt and pepper
250 g (9 oz) wholemeal pastry,
　defrosted if frozen
beaten egg, to glaze

Melt the butter in a large heavy saucepan over a moderate heat. Add the rabbit and cook until lightly browned. Add the onion and cook gently for 3-5 minutes until softened but not browned. Stir the flour into the pan juices. Gradually blend in the stock. Cover the pan and simmer for 10 minutes.

Add the lemon rind, lemon juice, carrot and herbs. Replace the cover and continue to simmer for 15 minutes.

Stir in the mushrooms and cream. Season to taste and cook for 5 minutes more. Divide the mixture between 4 individual pie dishes and allow to cool slightly while preparing the pastry lids.

Heat the oven to 200°C, 400°F, Gas Mark 6.

Divide the pastry into 4 equal portions. Roll each one out and use to cover the pies. Trim the edges using the pastry trimmings to decorate the tops of the pies. Brush the pies with beaten egg and cook in the oven for 25 minutes or until the pastry is golden.

Serving idea: Serve the pies with green cabbage or broccoli.

move the pan from the heat.

Drain the pasta and peas well. Return the pasta to the pan with the peas and the ham and cream mixture. Mix together for 3 minutes over a low heat to warm through. To serve, transfer to a serving dish and sprinkle with the Parmesan cheese.

Serving idea: Serve the pasta with a mixed green salad, crusty bread and a dry Italian wine.

Pork with green peppercorn sauce

SERVES 4-5
2100 Kj (500 Calories) per portion
30 g fat per portion

750 g (1½ lb) pork fillet, thinly
sliced
15 g (½ oz) butter
1 tbls sunflower oil
1 onion, finely chopped
1 clove garlic, crushed
100 g (4 oz) mushrooms, sliced
250 ml (8 fl oz) chicken stock
1 tsp French mustard
1 tbls green peppercorns in brine
142 ml (5 fl oz) carton soured cream
2 tsp cornflour
salt and pepper
snipped chives

Heat the butter and oil in a frying pan over a medium heat. Add the pork and cook until lightly browned. Reduce the heat, add the onion and garlic and cook for 5 minutes until soft but not browned. Stir in the mushrooms, stock and mustard. Cover and simmer for 12 minutes.

Crush the peppercorns slightly and stir them into the pork with the cream. Add the cornflour, blended with a little water. Season to taste, and cook gently for 3 minutes to heat through. Transfer to a serving dish and sprinkle with chives.

Serving idea: Serve with green beans and new potatoes.

Pasta with ham and peas

SERVES 4
1710 Kj (410 Calories) per portion
16 g fat per portion

250 g (9 oz) pasta twists
salt
1 tbls oil
175 g (6 oz) frozen peas
2 egg yolks
142 ml (5 fl oz) carton single cream
pinch of nutmeg
pepper
175 g (6 oz) lean ham cut into strips
15 g (½ oz) grated Parmesan
cheese

Bring a large pan of salted water to the boil. Add the oil and pasta and boil for 10 minutes, or until just tender.

Place the frozen peas in a bowl, pour boiling water over them and leave to stand. In a small saucepan beat together the egg yolks and cream. Season with nutmeg, salt and pepper. Add the ham. Heat gently, stirring constantly, until the mixture just starts to thicken. Re-

Pork dijonnaise

SERVES 4
2200 Kj (525 Calories) per portion
30 g fat per portion

750 g (1½ lb) pork fillet, trimmed
salt and pepper
2 tbls plain flour
3 tbls vegetable oil
50 ml (2 fl oz) dry vermouth
450 ml (¾ pint) chicken or ham
  stock
142 ml (5 fl oz) carton single cream
2 tbls Dijon mustard
pinch of grated nutmeg
For the julienne of vegetables
2 courgettes
2 medium carrots, scrubbed
1 medium parsnip, peeled
1 stick celery
½ medium onton

First prepare the julienne by cutting the courgettes, carrots, parsnip and celery into thin strips the size of matchsticks. Set them aside. Chop the vegetable trimmings very finely with the half-onion. Reserve separately.

Cut the pork into 2.5 cm (1 inch) thick slices and coat evenly with seasoned flour. Reserve any flour not covering the meat. Heat the oil in a frying pan over a moderate heat. Brown the pork lightly on all sides. Remove the pork from the pan and keep it warm. Place the chopped vegetable trimmings in the pan, season and cook gently for 3 minutes. Replace the pork, add the vermouth and simmer for 1 minute. Sprinkle over the remaining flour and stir it in. Add the stock, bring it to the boil and simmer gently for 15 minutes.

Meanwhile, steam the julienne of vegetables for 10-15 minutes until just soft. Lift the cooked pork with a slotted spoon on to a plate. Keep it warm and covered. Strain all the cooking juices into a saucepan, pushing any vegetables through as much as possible.

Set the pan over a high heat and boil until the sauce is reduced by half, and has a thick and creamy consistency. Reduce the heat and add the cream. Heat through without boiling. Stir in the mustard, combining it well. Add the nutmeg.

Return the pork to the pan and warm it through, without boiling over a gentle heat, so that the pork absorbs the flavour of the sauce. If the sauce is too thick, add a little milk. Transfer to a warmed dish to serve and arrange the julienne of vegetables over the top.

Serving idea: Serve with brown rice or with tiny new potatoes. The dish does not require additional vegetables as the julienne provides sufficient. It can be accompanied by a salad.

Meatball batter surprise

SERVES 4
1360 Kj (325 Calories) per portion
12 g fat per portion

For the batter
100 g (4 oz) plain flour
½ tsp salt
½ tsp dried mixed herbs
1 large egg
300 ml (½ pint) skimmed milk
For the meatballs
450 g (1 lb) lean minced beef
1 small onion, grated
50 g (2 oz) wholemeal
  breadcrumbs
1 tsp Worcestershire sauce
1 tbls tomato purée
salt and pepper
plain flour, for dusting
2 tbls sunflower oil

Heat the oven to 220°C, 425°F, Gas Mark 7.

To make the batter, sift the flour and salt into a bowl and sprinkle in the herbs. Make a well in the centre. Beat the egg lightly with 2 tablespoons of milk and pour into the well. Continue to beat the egg and milk, drawing the flour into the liquid and gradually adding the remainder of the milk. Beat well until the batter is quite smooth. Set aside while making the meatballs.

Place an ovenproof dish in the oven to heat.

Put the mince into a bowl with the onion, breadcrumbs, Worcestershire sauce and tomato purée. Season to taste. Combine these ingredients together and divide the mixture into 16 balls. Roll the meatballs in a little flour.

Heat the oil in a large frying pan over a moderate heat. Add the meatballs and fry, turning them gently in the fat until sealed. Transfer the meatballs to the ovenproof dish with any fat remaining in the pan. Quickly pour the batter around. Place the dish in the oven and cook for 35-40 minutes, until the batter is well risen and golden brown.

Serve immediately straight from the dish.

Serving idea: As this is quite a filling dish, all that is needed is a vegetable accompaniment such as carrots.

● Pork dijonnaise; Meatball batter surprise

Bobotie

SERVES 4

1860 Kj (445 Calories) per portion
22 g fat per portion

450 g (1 lb) minced beef or lamb
1 onion, finely chopped
1 tbls oil
1 clove garlic, crushed
3 tsp curry powder
1 dessert apple, peeled and
   chopped
50 g (2 oz) sultanas
1 tbls chutney
25 g (1 oz) wholemeal
   breadcrumbs
salt and pepper
2 eggs
300 ml (½ pint) semi-skimmed
   milk
25 g (1 oz) flaked almonds
3 bay leaves

Heat the oven to 180°C, 350°F, Gas Mark 4.

Put the minced beef or lamb into a large pan with the onion and oil. Cook over a moderate heat until the meat is browned and crumbly. Drain off any excess fat.

Add the garlic, curry powder and apple to the pan and cook for a further 2 minutes, stirring all the time. Mix in the sultanas, chutney and breadcrumbs and season to taste. Turn into a greased ovenproof dish.

Beat together the eggs and milk and pour over the meat mixture. Scatter over the almonds and place the bay leaves on top. Bake in the oven for 45 minutes or until the custard is set golden on top. Serve.

Serving idea: Serve with boiled potatoes and a green salad.

Marinated lamb kebabs

SERVES 4
1150 Kj (275 Calories) per portion
10 g fat per portion

450 g (1 lb) boned leg of lamb,
cubed
8 dried apricots
8 button onions
1 tbls chopped mint
lemon wedges, to garnish
For the marinade
2 × 150 g (5.29 oz) cartons natural
yoghurt
2 tbls finely chopped root ginger or
2 tsp ground ginger
1 clove garlic, crushed
1 tbls lemon juice
½ tsp ground coriander
1 tsp ground cumin
pinch cayenne pepper
salt and pepper

Mix all the ingredients for the marinade together in a shallow dish and season to taste. Add the lamb pieces and stir until they are well coated. Cover and leave in a cool place for 6 hours.

Place the apricots in a bowl and cover with boiling water. Leave them to soak while the lamb is marinating.

Lift the lamb out of the marinade with a slotted spoon. Drain the apricots. Thread the cubes of meat on to skewers alternately with the onions and apricots. Heat the grill to medium high and cook the kebabs for 12-15 minutes, turning them frequently.

Pour the marinade into a small saucepan over a low heat and warm it gently through. Stir in the mint.

Serve the kebabs garnished with lemon wedges. Hand the mint sauce separately in a jug or sauceboat.

Serving idea: Serve the kebabs with plain boiled rice cooked with a little lemon juice and zest.

Caribbean fish curry

SERVES 4
980 Kj (235 Calories) per portion
10 g fat per portion

750 g (1½ lb) cod fillet, skinned
2 tbls sunflower oil
1 tsp finely chopped root ginger
1 green chilli, seeded and finely
chopped
1 onion, finely chopped
1 clove garlic, crushed
1 tsp turmeric
2 tsp ground coriander
1 tsp grated lime rind
2 tbls lime juice
150 g (5.29 oz) carton coconut
yoghurt
pinch of salt and pepper
lime slices, to garnish

Cut the fish into large bite-size pieces.

Heat the oil in a large frying pan over a medium heat. Add the ginger and chilli and cook for 10 seconds. Add the onion and garlic and cook for 3 minutes until the onion is softened but not browned.

Stir in the turmeric and coriander and cook for 1 minute. Add the lime rind, lime juice, the pieces of fish and yoghurt and salt and pepper and cook gently for 10 minutes, stirring occasionally. Be very careful not to break up the fish.

When the fish is cooked, lift it out on to a warm serving plate. Let the sauce simmer for 1 minute. Pour it over the fish and serve garnished with slices of lime.

Serving idea: Serve with boiled rice and a carrot salad dressed with lime juice and mustard seed or a banana and coconut relish.

• Bobotie; Marinated lamb kebabs; Caribbean fish curry

Cod with watercress sauce

SERVES 4
670 Kj (160 Calories) per portion
5 g fat per portion

4 cod steaks, about 2 cm (¾ inch)
  thick
2 tsp lemon juice
15 g (½ oz) butter or margarine
3 tsp cornflour
300 ml (½ pint) semi-skimmed
  milk
½ fish stock cube
1 bunch watercress, trimmed and
  finely chopped
pepper
lemon twists, to garnish

Heat the grill to medium-hot.

Sprinkle the cod steaks with the lemon juice and dot with butter or margarine. Place under the grill and cook for 5-7 minutes on each side, depending on thickness.

Meanwhile, blend the cornflour with 1 or 2 teaspoons of the milk to make a smooth creamy paste. Put the rest of the milk into a saucepan with the stock cube over a moderate heat, and heat, stirring occasionally, until the cube dissolves. Stir in the blended cornflour and continue to cook until the sauce thickens. Reduce the heat, add the watercress and continue to cook for 2 minutes. Season with pepper if needed.

To serve, transfer the cod to one or two serving dishes. Pour over the sauce and garnish with twists of lemon.

Serving idea: Serve with new potatoes and a green vegetable.

Variation: Use haddock or Greenland halibut fillets if preferred.

● **Cod with watercrsss sauce; Fish and fennel hotpot**

Fish and fennel hotpot

SERVES 4
1740 Kj (415 Calories) per portion
12 g fat per portion

350 g (12 oz) Greenland halibut
  fillets, skinned
350 g (12 oz) huss, boned
750 g (1½ lb) potatoes, sliced
2 tbls lemon juice
salt and pepper
1 fennel bulb, thinly sliced
100 g (4 oz) mushrooms, sliced
25 g (1 oz) butter
25 g (1 oz) plain flour
300 ml (½ pint) semi-skimmed
  milk
1 tsp Dijon mustard
50 g (2 oz) half-fat Cheddar cheese

Heat the oven to 200°C, 400°F, Gas
Mark 6.
  Cut all the fish into 2.5 cm (1
inch) pieces. Put the sliced potatoes
in a saucepan and cover with water.
Bring to the boil and cook for 5
minutes. Drain the potato slices and
arrange half of them on the bottom

of a lightly greased medium ovenproof casserole. Cover with half of
the fish, sprinkle with 1 tablespoon
of the lemon juice and season to
taste. Add the fennel and
mushrooms. Place the remaining
fish on top and pour over the remaining lemon juice.
  Melt half of the butter in a small
saucepan over a moderate heat. Stir
in the flour and cook for 1 minute.
Gradually blend in the milk. Reduce
the heat, and continue to cook,
stirring all the time. Stir in the
mustard and cheese. When the
sauce has thickened, pour it over
the fish. Cover with the rest of the
potato slices. In a clean pan, melt
the remaining butter and brush it
over the potatoes. Cook in the oven
for 40 minutes.

Serving idea: Serve with a green
vegetable.

Variation: Other varieties of fish
may be used, as long as they have
firm flesh such as cod, haddock or
monkfish.

Vichyssoise

SERVES 4
1045 Kj (250 Calories) per portion
12 g fat per portion

25 g (1 oz) butter
450 g (1 lb) leeks, cleaned and
    chopped
350 g (12 oz) potatoes, sliced
1 small onion, finely chopped
600 ml (1 pint) chicken stock
600 ml (1 pint) milk
salt and pepper
To garnish
2 tbls single cream
snipped chives

Melt the butter in a large pan over a moderate heat. Add the vegetables and cook gently for 10 minutes, stirring occasionally to prevent sticking.

Add the stock and the milk. Bring to a simmer, cover the pan and cook for 20 minutes until the vegetables are quite tender. Allow to cool slightly, then sieve or pureé in a blender or food processor until smooth. Season to taste. Transfer to a tureen or individual soup bowls and leave to chill. Serve with a swirl of cream and a sprinkling of snipped chives.

• Vichyssoise;
Asparagus with mousseline sauce

Asparagus with mousseline sauce

This recipe incorporates a quick way of making hollandaise sauce in a food processor which gives it an especially light texture.

SERVES 6
974 Kj (233 Calories) per portion
24 g fat per portion

700 g (1½ lb) asparagus, fresh or
  frozen
For the sauce
175 g (6 oz) unsalted butter
2 eggs
2 tbls lemon juice
pepper
2 tbls whipping cream, whipped

If using fresh asparagus, trim the stalks then tie them in a neat bundle with fine string. Place them in a pan of simmering water and cook for about 10 minutes, or until tender, depending on the thickness of the stems. Drain. Remove the string, place the stems on a warmed serving plate. Keep warm. Cook frozen asparagus for 6-7 minutes.

To make the sauce, melt the butter in a small saucepan over a low heat. Put the eggs and lemon juice into a blender or food processor and turn on. Gradually pour the hot melted butter on to the eggs, blending all the time until the sauce thickens. If the butter is not hot enough the sauce may not be thick enough. In this case return the sauce to the pan and heat over the lowest heat, stirring all the time, until it thickens.

Season to taste with pepper. Fold in the cream and serve immediately with the asparagus.

Variation: This sauce is also good with hot or cold artichokes.

Quenelles de poisson with Sauce Nantua

This recipe does take a bit of time and care but is well worth the effort.

SERVES 4
1460 Kj (350 Calories) per portion
27 g fat per portion

For the quenelles
250 g (9 oz) fresh coley or haddock
3 egg whites
salt and pepper
pinch of ground mace
150 ml (¼ pint) low fat double
cream
For the sauce
225 g (8 oz) 'shell on' prawns
40 g (1½ oz) butter, softened
25 g (1 oz) plain flour
300 ml (½ pint) vegetable stock
150 ml (¼ pint) semi-skimmed
milk
150 ml (¼ pint) single cream
2 tsp lemon juice
strips lemon zest
12 peeled prawns, to garnish

Remove all the skin and bones from the fish. Chop the flesh roughly. Mince with the egg whites in a food processor or blender or pound thoroughly in a pestle and mortar until very smooth. Season with salt, pepper and mace. Gradually add the cream, but do not process for more than 20 seconds to prevent curdling. Press the mixture through a sieve and chill.

To make the sauce, separate the shells from the prawns. Discard the eyes and roes and place the shells in a liqidizer or food processor with the butter. Process for about 30 seconds until finely chopped. Scrape the mixture into a metal sieve and, using a wooden spoon, work the butter through the sieve into a pan. Discard the shells. Melt the butter over a low heat, blend in the flour

and cook gently for 2 minutes. Cool slightly. Add the stock and milk.

Set the pan over a moderate heat and cook gently for 2 minutes. Cool slightly before adding the stock and milk.

Set the pan over a moderate heat and whisk continually until the sauce reaches boiling point. Leave to simmer for 2-3 minutes. Stir in the cream to make a thin coating consistency. A little extra milk may be needed if the sauce is too thick. Keep the sauce warm and covered with clingfilm in a bain-marie (or in a container set in a roasting pan with simmering water half way up the sides of the container).

To cook the quenelles, bring a large shallow pan of water to the boil then turn down the heat so that the water is barely moving. Heat the oven to 140°C, 275°F, Gas Mark 1. Using 2 dessertspoons dipped in warm water, form the quenelles mixture into neat oval shapes and lower them gently into the water. Poach each one for about 10 minutes until just firm, turning once. Lift on to absorbent kitchen paper to drain and transfer immediately to a gratin dish. Leave enough space between each one for easy serving. Cover the dish with foil and keep warm in the oven.

Check the flavour, consistency and temperature of the sauce. Add the peeled prawns and lemon juice. Heat the sauce through without boiling. Spoon it over the quenelles. The sauce should flow over them freely, without being too thick or drowning them. Serve immediately before the sauce discolours or forms a skin.

Variation: For a very special occasion, replace white fish with fresh salmon. The tissues of frozen fish are broken down so may not hold the cream and egg whites so well.

• **Quenelles de poisson with Sauce Nantua; Oeufs portugaise**

Oeufs portugaise

SERVES 4
840 Kj (200 Calories) per portion
12 g fat per portion

15 g (½ oz) butter
1 small clove garlic, crushed
4 ripe tomatoes, skinned
salt and pepper
4 eggs, size 2, hard-boiled
1 tbls freshly chopped parsley
1 pinch dried marjoram
100 g (4 oz) carton low-fat soft
   cheese with garlic and herbs
flat leaf parsley, to garnish
For the sauce
15 g (½ oz) plain flour
pinch of dried mustard
300 ml (½ pint) skimmed milk
25 g (1 oz) mature cheddar,
   grated

Heat the oven to 200°C, 400°F, Gas Mark 6.

Melt the butter in a frying pan, over a moderate heat. Add the crushed garlic and cook for 1 minute. Cut the tomatoes into thick slices and sauté them in the garlic butter over a high heat for about 2 minutes on each side. Lift the tomato slices into 1 medium or 4 individual gratin dishes and season with salt and pepper. Reserve the juices from the pan.

Slice the eggs lengthways and scoop out the yolks. Press the yolks through a wire sieve with your thumb and blend the sieved yolk with the herbs and soft cheese. Fill the eggs with this mixture and arrange them on top of the tomatoes.

To make the sauce, heat the reserved juice in a small pan over a moderate heat. Stir in the flour and mustard and cook for 1 minute. Blend in the milk. Bring to the boil, stirring all the time. Reduce the heat and simmer gently for 3 minutes. Remove the pan from the heat and beat in half the cheese. It is important to use dry mature cheddar or the fat will be released during baking and make the dish oily. Coat each egg with sauce, sprinkle with the remaining cheese and bake in the oven for 10 minutes until golden brown. Garnish and serve.

Coronation chicken

SERVES 4-6
1710 Kj (410 Calories) per portion
20 g fat per portion

1.5 kg (3½ lb) chicken
1 onion
1 carrot, chopped
1 bay leaf
5 peppercorns
For the dressing
4 tbls mayonnaise
150 g (5.29 oz) carton natural
*   yoghurt*
1 tsp curry paste
1 tbls lemon juice
To garnish
small seedless grapes
1 dessert apple, cored and sliced
paprika

Place the chicken in a large saucepan with the onion, carrot, bay leaf and peppercorns. Add just enough water to cover the chicken. Place the pan over a moderate heat and simmer for about 50 minutes, or until the chicken is just tender. Leave it to cool in the stock.

Lift the cold chicken out of the saucepan, reserving the stock for soup. Remove all the skin from the chicken and cut the meat from the carcass. Cut it into large bite-size pieces and arrange them on a serving dish.

In a bowl mix together the mayonnaise, yoghurt, curry paste and lemon juice. Spoon this dressing over the chicken. To serve, garnish with grapes and slices of apple and sprinkle paprika on top.

Serving idea: Serve with a rice salad, a green salad or a bean salad.

Variation: Left-over cold turkey makes a good substitute for the chicken.

Chicken in tarragon sauce

SERVES 4
1440 Kj (345 Calories) per portion
17 g fat per portion

1.5 kg (3½ lb) chicken
900 ml (1½ pints) weak chicken
  stock
2 carrots, roughly chopped
2 celery sticks, chopped
1 bouquet garni
For the sauce
25 g (1 oz) butter
25 g (1 oz) plain flour
1 tbls chopped tarragon
4 tbls single cream
salt and pepper
To garnish
fresh tarragon leaves
small cooked carrots

Place the chicken in a large flameproof casserole with the stock, carrots, celery and bouquet garni. Set the casserole over a moderate heat and bring it slowly to the boil. Cover the casserole and poach the chicken for 1 hour or until it is cooked.

Remove the chicken from the liquid and cut it into 4 portions. Remove the skin and place the chicken on a heated serving dish. Set aside to keep warm. Strain the cooking liquid into a saucepan. Let it boil until it is reduced to 450 ml (¾ pint).

To make the sauce, melt the butter in a small pan over a moderate heat. Add the flour, and cook for 2 minutes. Gradually stir in the reduced stock and the chopped tarragon. Bring to the boil. Reduce the heat and simmer until the sauce thickens. Stir in the cream and simmer gently. Season to taste.

To serve, spoon the sauce over the chicken and garnish with sprigs of tarragon and small carrots.

Pork and lime sauté

SERVES 4
1690 Kj (405 Calories) per portion
20 g fat per portion

450 g (1 lb) thick pork fillet
salt and pepper
15 g (½ oz) fresh root ginger
15 g (½ oz) butter
2 tbls olive oil
rind and juice of 1 lime
250 ml (8 fl oz) chicken stock
3 tbls double cream
To garnish
1 kiwi fruit, peeled and sliced
1 lime, sliced

Using a sharp knife, cut the pork into 12 pieces. Place them between sheets of clingfilm and beat them to half their original thickness. Season to taste.

Cut the ginger into fine strips. Put them in a small bowl and cover with boiling water for 1 minute to blanch them. Drain and set aside.

Heat the butter and oil in a large frying pan over a moderate heat. Fry the pork for 8 minutes, turning the slices once. Remove the pork from the pan and keep warm.

Add the ginger to the pan, with the lime rind and juice and the stock. Raise the heat and boil until the liquid is reduced by half. Stir in the cream and season to taste.

Pour a little of the sauce on to 4 warm dinner plates. Arrange 3 pieces of pork on each. Halve the kiwi slices and place a piece on each portion of pork. Garnish the plate with a twist of lime and serve.

Serving idea: Serve with new potatoes, julienne of carrots and mange tout.

● Coronation chicken; Chicken in tarragon sauce; Pork and lime sauté

Veal Sylvie

SERVES 4
1380 Kj (330 Calories) per portion
18 g fat per portion

4 × 150 g (5 oz) veal escalopes
salt and pepper
4 slices mild cured ham
75 g (3 oz) Gruyère cheese, grated
25 g (1 oz) butter
120 ml (4 fl oz) dry white wine
1 tsp freshly chopped sage
2 tbls soured cream
sage leaves, to garnish

Heat the oven to 190°C, 375°F, Gas Mark 5. Place each escalope between sheets of clingfilm and beat out until very thin. Cut in half and season.

Cut each slice of ham in half. Place a piece on each portion of veal. Divide the cheese between each portion. Roll them up and secure with a cocktail stick.

Heat the butter in a frying pan over a moderate heat. Sauté the veal rolls until golden, and transfer to a shallow ovenproof dish. Add the wine and sage. Cover and cook in the oven for 30 minutes, turning them over half-way during cooking.

Stir in the soured cream and serve garnished with sage leaves.

Serving idea: Serve with new potatoes and a green vegetable.

Variation: Use pork escalopes if preferred and beat out in the same way.

Steak au poivre

SERVES 4
1460 Kj (350 Calories) per portion
15 g fat per portion

4 × 150 g (5 oz) fillet steaks, about
  2.5 cm (1 inch) thick
vegetable oil
2 tbls black peppercorns, coarsely
  crushed
15 g (½ oz) butter
1 shallot, finely chopped
1 tbls brandy
150 ml (¼ pint) dry white wine
3 tbls double cream
salt
watercress to garnish

Heat the grill to high.

Brush the steaks with oil. Press the crushed peppercorns on to each side. Place under the hot grill and cook for approximately 4-5 minutes on each side or according to how well done you like your steak.

Meanwhile, melt the butter in a saucepan and gently cook the shallot for 5 minutes until golden and soft. Pour in the brandy, bring it quickly to the boil, then reduce the heat and let it simmer for 2 minutes. Repeat this process with the wine, letting it boil for 5 minutes to reduce the sauce slightly. Stir in the cream and heat it through without boiling. Season with salt.

To serve, place a steak on each plate, pour a little sauce over, and garnish with watercress.

Serving idea: Serve with jacket potatoes and a mixed salad.

• Veal Sylvie;
Steak au poivre;
Fricassee of lamb

Fricassee of lamb

SERVES 4
2090 Kj (500 Calories) per portion
25 g fat per portion

750 g (1½ lb) boned leg of lamb
25 g (1 oz) butter
1 tbls oil
1 Spanish onion, chopped
4 large carrots, sliced
2 tbls plain flour
600 ml (1 pint) chicken stock
150 ml (¼ pint) dry white wine
1 bouquet garni
salt and pepper
225 g (8 oz) button mushrooms,
*   stalks trimmed*
2 egg yolks
142 ml (5 fl oz) single cream
chopped parsley and parsley sprig,
*   to garnish*

Cut the lamb into neat cubes, discarding all the fat. In a large saucepan over a moderate heat, melt the butter with the oil. Sauté the lamb until lightly browned on all sides. Remove with a slotted spoon and set aside.

Add the onion and carrots to the pan and cook until the onion is transparent and the carrot golden. Sprinkle the flour into the pan and stir until a pale roux forms. Gradually stir in the stock and wine. Bring to the boil, stirring all the time. Return the meat to the pan with the bouquet garni. Season to taste, cover and simmer gently for 1¼-1½ hours or until the lamb is tender. Add the mushrooms 15 minutes before the end of cooking time.

In a bowl whisk the egg yolks with the cream. Ladle a little of the hot sauce from the lamb into the cream mixture, whisking all the time. Pour the egg and cream mixture into the casserole and stir well. Do not allow it to boil. Garnish with parsley.

Serving idea: Serve with boiled rice, noodles or baked potatoes.

Plaice rolls with prawn sauce

SERVES 4
1090 Kj (260 Calories) per portion
9 g fat per portion

6 medium plaice fillets, skinned
150 ml (¼ pint) fish stock
150 ml (¼ pint) dry white wine
25 g (1 oz) butter
25 g (1 oz) plain flour
1 tsp tomato purée
1 tsp lemon juice
50 g (2 oz) peeled prawns
4 tbls double cream
salt and pepper
50 g (2 oz) peeled prawns, to
   garnish

Heat the oven to 180°C, 350°F, Gas Mark 4.

Cut the plaice fillets in half lengthways. Roll each piece up starting at the narrow end. Place them side by side in an ovenproof dish with the seam underneath. Pour over the stock and wine, cover and bake in the oven for 15 minutes. Carefully strain the liquor from the cooked fish and keep them warm.

To make the sauce, melt the butter in a small saucepan over a moderate heat. Add the flour and cook for 2 minutes. Remove the pan from the heat and gradually stir in the fish liquor. Set the pan back on the heat, and bring the sauce slowly to the boil, stirring continuously. Stir in the tomato purée and lemon juice. Pour the sauce into a blender, add the prawns and purée until smooth. Return to the pan, stir in the cream and season to taste.

To serve, spoon the sauce over the fish rolls and garnish with prawns and lemon slices.

Serving idea: Serve with new potatoes and petit pois.

Sole bonne femme

SERVES 4
773 Kj (185 Calories) per portion
8 g fat per portion

8 medium lemon sole fillets
100 g (4 oz) mushrooms, sliced
1 shallot, finely chopped
1 tbls chopped parsley
salt and pepper
1 tbls lemon juice
150 ml (¼ pint) dry white wine
15 g (½ oz) butter
1 tbls plain flour
1 egg yolk
1 tbls single cream
pinch of cayenne pepper
To garnish
lemon wedges
parsley sprigs (optional)

Heat the oven to 180°C, 350°F, Gas Mark 4.

Place the mushrooms, shallot and parsley in the bottom of an ovenproof dish. Season the fish. Fold the fillets in half and place them in the dish. Sprinkle with the lemon juice and pour over the wine. Cover the dish and cook in the oven for 20 minutes.

Lift the cooked fish on to a warm serving dish to keep hot. Strain the cooking liquid into a small saucepan, reserving the mushrooms. Work the butter and flour together with a fork to make a paste. Place the pan of liquid over a gentle heat, and as it cooks add small spoonfuls of the paste, whisking all the time.

Blend the egg yolk and cream together in a small bowl. Whisk them into the sauce, making sure it does not boil. Add the reserved mushrooms to warm through. Season the sauce to taste. Add the cayenne pepper and pour it over the fish. Serve at once, garnished with lemon wedges, and parsley if using.

Serving idea: Serve with broccoli, mange tout or fine green beans.

● Normandy fish; Plaice rolls with prawn sauce; Sole bonne femme

Normandy fish

SERVES 4
1045 Kj (250 Calories) per portion
9 g fat per portion

4 × 175 g (6 oz) thick cod steaks or
*   fillets*
25 g (1 oz) butter
250 ml (8 fl oz) dry cider
2 carrots, cut into thin strips
1 leek, cut into 5 cm (2 inch)
*   lengths and shredded*
1 tbls flour
salt and pepper
3 tbls single cream

Heat the oven to 180°C, 350°F, Gas Mark 4. Using a little of the butter, grease an ovenproof dish. Arrange the fish in one layer and pour over 150 ml (¼ pint) of the cider. Cover and cook in the oven for 15 minutes.

Meanwhile put half of the remaining butter into a small saucepan with the carrots and leek. Cover the pan and place it over a moderate heat. Allow the vegetables to sweat for 10 minutes until just tender.

Remove the fish from the oven. Lift the pieces on to a hot serving dish, and spoon over the vegetables. Return the dish to the oven to keep warm. Pour the cooking liquid into a saucepan with the rest of the cider and simmer for 2-3 minutes to reduce a little.

Melt the remaining butter in a small pan. Stir in the flour and cook for 1 minute. Add the sauce, stirring constantly, bring to the boil, then reduce heat. Season to taste. Stir in the cream and heat through. Pour the sauce over the fish and serve.

DESSERTS

These tempting desserts are classics to be dipped into for special occasions. The Strawberry gâteau and French fruit tart would also make impressive fare for a coffee morning.

French fruit tart

SERVES 8
1670 Kj (400 Calories) per portion
22 g fat per portion

For the pastry
200 g (7 oz) plain flour
150 g (5 oz) butter or block
  margarine
2 tbls caster sugar
1 egg yolk, beaten
2-3 tsp milk or water
For the filling
2 egg yolks
50 g (2 oz) caster sugar
40 g (1½ oz) plain flour
300 ml (½ pint) Breakfast (Jersey)
  milk
25 g (1 oz) ground almonds
1-2 drops of almond essence
100 g (4 oz) strawberries, halved
1 kiwi fruit, sliced and halved
150 g (6 oz) black grapes
50 g (2 oz) green grapes
For the glaze
4 tbls apricot jam
1 tbls lemon juice
1 tbls brandy or almond liqueur

To make the pastry, sieve the flour into a mixing bowl, and rub in the butter or margarine until the mixture resembles fine breadcrumbs. Stir in the sugar. Work in the beaten egg yolk to make a dough. Add water or milk if needed. Knead lightly, wrap in cling film and refrigerate for 1 hour.

Heat the oven to 200°C, 400°F, Gas Mark 6.

Roll the pastry out on a floured surface and use it to line a 23 cm (9 inch) flan tin. Prick the pastry with a fork, cover it with foil and fill with baking beans. Place it in the oven and bake blind for 15 minutes. Remove the foil and beans and continue to bake for a further 10 minutes until the pastry shell is crisp and golden. Allow to cool in tin.

To make the filling, beat the egg yolks and sugar in a large bowl until they are pale. Add the flour. In a small pan, bring the milk to just under boiling point and pour it on to the egg mixture. Strain the mixture back into the pan and cook over a gentle heat, whisking all the time until a thick custard is formed. Remove the pan from the heat and stir in the almonds and essence. Pour the custard in to the flan case. Level the surface with a palette knife and leave to cool.

When the custard is cold, arrange the fruit, cut side down, on top, in decorative rows.

To make the glaze, put the jam in a saucepan with the lemon juice and brandy and simmer until the glaze becomes thick and syrupy. Brush the glaze over the fruit, and leave to cool and set.

Remove the flan from the tin and serve on a flat plate.

Strawberry gâteau

This unusual sponge is made with semolina and ground almonds and has a light, crunchy texture.

SERVES 8
1110 Kj (265 Calories) per portion
13 g fat per portion

flour, for dusting
5 eggs, separated
150 g (5 oz) caster sugar
1 tsp grated lemon rind
1 tbls lemon juice
100 g (4 oz) semolina
50 g (2 oz) ground almonds
For the filling
1 tbls rosewater
225 g (8 oz) strawberries, sliced
142 ml (5 fl oz) carton whipping cream
icing sugar, for dredging

Heat the oven to 180°C, 350°F, Gas Mark 4.

Grease and line the bases of two 20 cm (8 inch) sandwich tins. Grease the lining paper and dust with flour.

In a large bowl beat the egg yolks, sugar, lemon rind and juice until the mixture is thick and pale. Gradually beat in the semolina. When the mixture is smooth and very thick add the ground almonds.

Whisk the egg whites until they form stiff peaks. Carefully fold them into the mixture. Divide it evenly between the prepared tins and bake in the oven for 35 minutes until a skewer inserted in the centre of the cakes comes out clean.

To make the filling, pour the rosewater over the sliced strawberries. Leave them to marinate for 20 minutes. Strain the fruit, discarding the liquid.

Remove the cakes from the oven and leave in the tins to cool for 30 minutes.

Whip the cream and fold in the strawberries. Take the cakes out of the tins and sandwich them together with the fruit and cream. Dust the top with icing sugar.

● French fruit tart;
Strawberry gâteau

Fruity clafouti

SERVES 4-6
880 Kj (210 Calories) per portion
10 g fat per portion

700 g (1 1/4 lb) Victoria plums,
*   halved and stoned*
1 tbls lemon juice
1/4 tsp cinnamon
2 tsp caster sugar
For the batter
50 g (2 oz) self-raising flour
75 g (3 oz) caster sugar
2 eggs
25 g (1 oz) butter, melted
300 ml (1/2 pint) semi-skimmed
*   milk*
1/4 tsp almond essence
icing sugar for dusting

Heat the oven to 200°C, 400°F, Gas
Mark 6. Toss the halved plums in
lemon juice and place them in a
shallow ovenproof dish. Mix the cinnamon and sugar together and
sprinkle over the plums.

To make the batter, put the flour
and sugar into a large bowl. Make a
well in the centre and pour in the
eggs and butter. Beat well, gradually
adding the milk, and incorporating
the flour and sugar. When the mixture is smooth, add the almond
essence and beat again. Pour the
batter over the fruit and bake in the
oven for 30-35 minutes, or until set
and golden.

Serve immediately dusted with
icing sugar.

Pears sabayon

SERVES 4-6
860 Kj (205 Calories) per portion
4 g fat per portion

4 large firm ripe dessert pears
juice of 1/2 lemon
85 ml (3 fl oz) Marsala
2 egg yolks
50 g (2 oz) caster sugar
1 tbls brandy

Heat the oven to 180°C, 350°F, Gas Mark 4.

Half fill a bowl with water and add the lemon juice. Peel, halve and core the pears. Place them in the water to prevent discoloration during preparation.

Drain the pears and arrange them cut side down in a baking dish. Pour over the Marsala, cover the dish and cook for 20-25 minutes or until the pears are tender.

Transfer the pears to a serving dish, reserving the cooking liquid. Place the egg yolks and sugar in a bowl and whisk until the mixture is pale and frothy. Add the juice from the pears. Place the bowl over a pan of simmering water and whisk until the mixture is thick and foamy. Stir in the brandy. Pour the sauce over the pears and serve immediately.

● Fruity clafouti;
Pears sabayon;
Pashka

Pashka

SERVES 8
1230 Kj (295 Calories) per portion
24 g fat per portion

450 g (1 lb) curd cheese
1 egg yolk
75 g (3 oz) caster sugar
½ tsp vanilla essence
85 ml (3 fl oz) double cream
50 g (2 oz) blanched almonds
50 g (2 oz) seedless raisins
To decorate
glacé fruit
angelica
whole blanched almonds

Line a 1 litre (1½ pint) basin with a double thickness of scalded muslin.

In a bowl beat the cheese, egg yolk, sugar and vanilla essence together until smooth. Lightly whip the cream and fold it into the cheese mixture with the almonds and raisins. Spoon into the prepared bowl and fold the cloth over. Cover with a saucer and place a weight on top. Place in the refrigerator and chill overnight.

Remove the weight and plate. Unfold the cloth and invert the pudding on to a serving plate. Peel away the muslin.

Decorate the top and sides with glacé fruit, angelica and almonds.

Vanilla ice-cream

SERVES 6
1360 Kj (325 Calories) per portion
24 g fat per portion

450 ml (¾ pint) milk
2 eggs
2 egg yolks
100 g (4 oz) caster sugar
½ tsp vanilla essence
284 ml (10 fl oz) carton whipping
*   cream*

In a small saucepan heat the milk almost to scalding. Beat the eggs, egg yolks, sugar and vanilla essence together in a bowl. Stir in the milk, stirring all the time. Strain the mixture back into the saucepan. Cook the custard gently over a low heat until it coats the back of a spoon. Do not allow the custard to boil. Pour into a shallow freezer container and leave to cool. When cool, freeze for about 2 hours until mushy.

Turn the frozen custard into a large bowl and whisk it up to break down the crystals. Lightly whip the cream and fold it into the custard mixture. Put the mixture back into the freezer container and freeze for 1 more hour. Remove and stir well. Freeze again until the ice-cream is firm.

Transfer the ice-cream to the refrigerator 20 minutes before serving to soften. Scoop into chilled glasses to serve.

Serving idea: Serve with wafer biscuits or langues de chat.

Variation: Chocolate ice-cream: break up 175 g (6 oz) plain chocolate into small pieces and melt it with the milk, stirring until smooth. Coffee ice-cream: dissolve 3 tablespoons of instant coffee in 2 tablespoons of boiling water and add to the cooked custard. Strawberry ice-cream: purée 350 g (12 oz) strawberries with 25 g (1 oz) icing sugar and stir into the cool custard.

Soufflé Grand Marnier

SERVES 6-8
1300 Kj (310 Calories) per portion
23 g fat per portion

15 g (½ oz) sachet powdered
*   gelatine*
5 large eggs, size 1 or 2, separated
100 g (4 oz) caster sugar
120 ml (4 fl oz) Grand Marnier
grated rind of 1 orange
284 ml (10 fl oz) carton whipping
*   cream*
To decorate
fine strips of orange rind
25 g (1 oz) toasted chopped
*   almonds*
orange segments

Using a length of string, tie a collar of double-layer greaseproof paper around a 1.2 litre (2 pint) soufflé dish so that it stands 5 cm (2 inches) above the rim.

Put 3 tbls of water in a small bowl. Sprinkle over the gelatine and leave it to soak for a few minutes. Stand the bowl in a pan of simmering water until dissolved.

Put the egg yolks and caster sugar into a bowl and whisk until light and creamy. Whisk in the Grand Marnier, orange rind and gelatine. In another bowl whip the cream until it is floppy. Fold into the egg mixture.

Whisk the egg whites until they form stiff peaks. Fold them into the soufflé mixture. Pour into the prepared soufflé dish and leave in the refrigerator to set for at least 4 hours.

To serve, remove the paper collar carefully, using a knife to ease it away from the soufflé.

Carefully press the nuts into the sides above the dish and arrange orange segments and strips of rind on the top, to decorate.

● **Vanilla ice-cream:**
Soufflé Grand Marnier

Profiteroles with fruit coulis

SERVES 6
1590 Kj (380 Calories) per portion
20 g fat per portion

50 g (2 oz) butter
150 ml (¼ pint) water
65 g (2½ oz) plain flour, sifted
2 eggs, beaten
200 ml (7 fl oz) whipping cream
2 tbls icing sugar
1 egg white
For the coulis
450 g (1 lb) frozen raspberries
50 g (2 oz) light brown sugar

Heat the oven to 220°C, 425°F, Gas Mark 7. Grease 2 baking sheets.

Put the butter and water into a saucepan and bring slowly to the boil. Take the pan quickly from the heat and add the flour all at once. Beat the mixture until it forms a smooth paste which leaves the sides of the pan. Allow to cool for a minute then gradually beat in the eggs. Continue to beat until the paste has a sheen.

Pipe or spoon small balls of the mixture on to the baking sheets. Bake in the oven for 15 minutes. Reduce the temperature to 200°C, 400°F, Gas Mark 6 and cook for a further 5 minutes until golden and crisp. Remove from the oven and make a small slit in each bun to allow the steam to escape while cooling.

To make the coulis, put the raspberries and sugar into a saucepan with 2 tbls water. Cook, covered, for about 10 minutes until the raspberries are soft. Sieve into a jug and set aside.

Whip the cream and icing sugar together in a bowl until firm. Whisk the egg white until it forms stiff peaks. Fold it into the cream. Fill the choux buns with this mixture, using piping bag or spoon, and serve on a dessert dish with the warm or cold raspberry sauce separately.

Gooseberry and almond whip

SERVES 4
840 Kj (200 Calories) per portion
12 g fat per portion

450 g (1 lb) gooseberries, topped
* and tailed*
2 tbls honey
50 g (2 oz) almonds, toasted and
* chopped*
225 g (8 oz) carton Greek-style
* yoghurt*
1 egg white
chopped almonds, to decorate

Put the gooseberries into a pan with the honey and 4 tablespoons of water. Cover the pan and cook over a low heat for 15-20 minutes until tender. Put the cooked gooseberries into a bowl and mash them.

When the fruit is cold, stir in the almonds and yoghurt. Whisk the egg white until it is stiff. Fold it into the fruit. Divide the mixture between four glasses. Chill for 1 hour. Decorate with chopped almonds to serve.

Redcurrant sponge drops

MAKES 10
480 Kj (115 Calories) per portion
6 g fat per portion

50 g (2 oz) caster sugar
2 eggs
few drops of vanilla essence
50 g (2 oz) plain flour
caster sugar, for sprinkling
For the filling
142 ml (5 fl oz) carton whipping
cream
1 tbls icing sugar
100 g (4 oz) redcurrants

Heat the oven to 190°C, 375°F, Gas Mark 5.

Whisk the sugar, eggs and vanilla essence together in a mixing bowl over a pan of hot water until the mixture is thick. Carefully fold in the flour. Place 20 dessertspoonfuls of the mixture on to floured baking sheets, dust with caster sugar and cook in the oven for 6-8 minutes until golden brown. Transfer to a wire rack to cool.

Whip the cream and icing sugar until thick. Place 1 spoonful on 10 of the sponge drops. Add a few redcurrants to each, and cover with the remaining drops. Sprinkle lightly with caster sugar to serve.

Variation: Blackcurrants or raspberries also make a good filling.

● Gooseberry and almond whip;
Profiteroles with fruit coulis;
Redcurrant sponge drops

Blackcurrant mousse

SERVES 6-8
670 Kj (160 Calories) per portion
8 g fat per portion

450 g (1 lb) blackcurrants, fresh or
frozen
50 g (2 oz) sugar
1 blackcurrant jelly
142 ml (5 fl oz) carton whipping
cream
2 egg whites
4 tbls whipped cream, to decorate
(optional)

Reserve a few whole blackcurrants
for decoration. Put the remainder in
a saucepan with the sugar and
2 tablespoons of water. Cover, and
cook gently until the fruit is soft.
Press through a sieve into a bowl.

Dissolve the jelly in 150 ml
(¼ pint) boiling water. Whisk it into
the blackcurrant purée. Allow to

cool, then refrigerate until the mixture begins to thicken.

Whip the cream until thick and
fold it into the fruit mixture. Whisk
the egg whites until they stand in
soft peaks. Fold them into the
mousse. Pour the mousse into a
glass serving bowl and refrigerate
until set. Decorate.

Plum and ginger fool

SERVES 4
670 Kj (160 Calories) per portion
2 g fat per portion

560 g (1 lb 6 oz) can Golden Plums
1 tbls stem ginger, chopped
2 tbls cornflour
450 ml (¾ pint) skimmed milk
25 g (1 oz) sugar
1 egg

Drain the plums and remove the

• Blackcurrant mousse;
Plum and ginger fool;
Hot buttered brandy

stones. Mash them with a fork in a bowl until pulpy. Stir in the ginger.

In a bowl, blend the cornflour with a little of the milk. Heat the rest of the milk to boiling point in a small pan. Pour the milk on to the blended cornflour, stirring constantly. Return the mixture to the pan and heat gently, stirring all the time as it thickens. Allow to simmer for 1 minute.

Whisk the sugar and egg together in a bowl. Slowly whisk the egg into the custard, continuing to cook until the custard becomes thick. Do not let it boil. Cool the custard then fold it gently into the fruit mixture, blending well. Chill until required.

Serve in individual glasses or a glass bowl.

Hot buttered brandy

SERVES 1
1170 Kj (280 Calories) per portion
13 g fat per portion

25 ml (1 fl oz) brandy
2 tsp clover honey
2.5 cm (1 inch) piece cinnamon stick
250 ml (8 fl oz) semi-skimmed milk
knob of butter
pinch of mixed spices

Place the brandy, honey and cinnamon stick in a warmed mug. In a small saucepan, heat the milk to boiling point and pour it into the mug, stirring to melt the honey. Cut the butter into several pieces and dot them over the top. Sprinkle with mixed spices and serve.

Variation: Substitute rum for brandy.

Hot chocolate and orange

SERVES 4
500 Kj (120 Calories) per portion
6 g fat per portion

*46 g (1¾ oz) bar orange milk
  chocolate
300 ml (½ pint) skimmed milk
2 eggs, size 1
grated nutmeg*

Break the chocolate into pieces and put them in a small saucepan with the milk. Bring to the boil, stirring constantly to melt the chocolate.

Place the eggs in a mixing bowl and stand over a pan of gently simmering water. Whisk either with a rotary or electric whisk and gradually pour in the chocolate milk. Continue to whisk over the hot water for 8-10 minutes until the mixture has thickened slightly and is very hot and frothy.

Pour into warmed cups and serve with a little grated nutmeg on top.

● Hot chocolate and orange; Irish coffee; Iced coffee; Tropical sunrise

Irish coffee

SERVES 1
1250 Kj (300 Calories) per portion
24 g fat per portion

*25 ml (1 fl oz) Irish Whiskey
2 sugar lumps
150 ml (¼ pint) very hot black
  coffee
50 ml (2 fl oz) double cream*

Pour hot water into a goblet glass with a stem to heat it. Drain and dry the glass. Place the sugar lumps in the bottom, cover with the whiskey and pour over the coffee. Stir well.

Hold a spoon poised near the surface of the coffee and pour the cream gently over it. Do not stir or allow the spoon to touch the coffee. The cool cream will stay on top of the hot coffee. Serve immediately.

Variation: A lower fat whipping cream could be used, providing it is lightly whipped before serving. Alter the amount of whiskey and cream in each glass, according to taste.

Iced coffee

SERVES 4
670 Kj (160 Calories) per portion
5 g fat per portion

1 heaped tbls soft, brown sugar
300 ml (½ pint) strong black coffee
300 ml (½ pint) semi-skimmed
 milk
142 ml (5 fl oz) carton half-cream

Add the sugar to the hot coffee in a bowl and stir until dissolved. Allow to cool. Stir in the milk. When completely cold, whisk in the cream. Pour into glasses and chill well before serving.

Variation: Each glass of coffee could be served with a tablespoon of single cream swirled on the top.

Tropical sunrise

SERVES 4
840 Kj (200 Calories) per portion
5 g fat per portion

425 g (15 oz) can apricots, drained,
 juice discarded
2 tbls lemon juice
4 tbls smatana
600 ml (1 pint) tropical fruit drink

Place the apricots and lemon juice in a blender and purée until smooth. Spoon the apricot purée into 4 glasses, cover with a layer of smatana and chill in the refrigerator for five minutes. Shake the fruit drink well and spoon some over the top of the smatana, being careful not to disturb the two layers. Finish each glass with crushed ice and serve with a straw.

Variation: When available, use fresh apricots poached in a light sugar syrup and lemon juice.

Banana and vanilla drink

SERVES 4
420 Kj (100 Calories) per portion
1 g fat per portion

*2 × 150 g (5.29 oz) cartons vanilla
yoghurt
600 ml (1 pint) skimmed milk
2 very ripe bananas, sliced*

Blend all the ingredients together in a liquidizer and serve immediately. If this is made in advance, the banana will discolour.

Variation: Try orange yoghurt or chocolate yoghurt for tasty variations on a theme.

Tomato and orange cocktail

SERVES 4
170 Kj (40 Calories) per portion
0 g fat per portion

*300 ml (½ pint) chilled tomato juice
juice of 2 large oranges
2 tbls fresh mint, very finely
chopped
150 g (5.29 oz) carton natural
yoghurt, to serve*

Combine the tomato juice with the freshly squeezed orange juice in a blender, or whisk together. Stir in the chopped mint. Serve the chilled mixture in glasses and swirl a tablespoon of lightly beaten yoghurt into each.

Strawberry milkshakes

This is an ideal way of using slightly mushy strawberries during the summer, or frozen strawberries at any time.

SERVES 4
400 Kj (95 Calories) per portion
2 g fat per portion

*275 g (10 oz) strawberries
450 ml (¾ pint) semi-skimmed
milk
4 scoops vanilla ice-cream*
To decorate
*1 egg white
1 tbls caster sugar
firm, small strawberries if
available
caster sugar for dredging*

Purée the strawberries in a blender. Strain into a bowl to give about 450 ml (¾ pint) purée. Return to the blender with the milk and ice-cream and blend thoroughly. Pour into 4 tall glasses and chill.

To serve, whisk the egg white with caster sugar until it forms stiff peaks. Dip the strawberries into the egg white. Dredge liberally with caster sugar. Place on a cooling rack to firm, then add to the top of the glass just before serving.

Variation: The themes are endless but lightly sugared raspberries combined with banana ice-cream make another delicious summer shake.

• **Strawberry milkshake; Banana and vanilla drink; Tomato and orange cocktail**

INDEX